Stop the Bullying

Stop the Bullying

A Handbook for Schools

Ken Rigby

Jessica Kingsley Publishers
London

First published in Australia in 2001 by
The Australian Council for Educational Research Limited

This edition published in the United Kingdom in 2002
by Jessica Kingsley Publishers Ltd
116 Pentonville Road
London N1 9JB, England
and
325 Chestnut Street
Philadelphia, PA 19106, USA

www.jkp.com

Copyright © 2001 Ken Rigby

British Library Cataloguing in Publication Data
A CIP catalogue record for this book is available from the British Library

ISBN 1 84310 070 3

Printed and Bound in Great Britain by
Athenaeum Press, Gateshead, Tyne and Wear

CONTENTS

ACKNOWLEDGMENTS

I am enormously indebted to the thousands of children, teachers and parents who, over the last 12 years, have shared with me their concerns about school bullying, their ideas about what can be done about it, and their heartfelt hope that there will come a day when bullying simply doesn't happen.

Then there are people who have kindly read through the text of this handbook and offered me good advice and encouragement.

Especially I would like to thank Ms Karen Kitchen, Student Attendance Counsellor – Special Projects, Education Department of South Australia; Ms Alison Soutter, Senior Education Officer, NSW Department of Education and Training; and Ms Jenny Blake, Acting Senior Education Officer, Student Services Branch, Education Services Directorate Education, Queensland, for their perceptive comments. Their expertise and working knowledge of the needs of school personnel in addressing the problem has been much appreciated. They have helped me to write a better book. However, they must not be held in any way accountable for any errors, misjudgments or personal opinions that may disturb or challenge the reader. These are mine and mine alone.

Ken Rigby

THE PURPOSE OF THE HANDBOOK

This handbook is to help us deal more effectively with the problem of bullying in schools. Those who educate about bullying include both teachers and parents. It is only through mutual understanding of each other's role and a joint resolve to work collaboratively with each other that the problem of bullying will ever be solved. Hence, although this handbook is directed primarily at informing educators in schools, I hope that it will be read also by parents who care about bullying in schools, who want to know what can be done about it, and who want to work closely with schools to help stop the bullying.

Since the 1970s there has been increasing attention paid to the problem throughout the world. In a major book on the subject published in 1999 titled *The Nature of Bullying* (edited by Peter Smith and others) there are accounts by researchers in 34 countries and from every continent of bullying in schools. Research on issues in school bullying continues to be published in refereed journals at an increasing rate. International and national conferences are now examining bullying as a central theme. It is not easy to keep up with this flow of information.

At the same time the issue of school bullying is a growing community concern. This is reflected in the importance that is being attached to the issue in the media. It is also evident in encouragement that is sometimes given to parents to take legal action against a school when they believe there has been a breach in the duty of care that schools have in protecting children from severe forms of peer bullying[1]. This may sometimes create a doomsday illusion that bullying is becoming ever more prevalent in an increasingly dysfunctional society. This is not the case. What is happening is that we are becoming more sensitive to the harm bullying can do, less into denial that it is happening, and generally more optimistic that bullying can be greatly reduced.

For several years now some progressive schools have been taking the matter very seriously and putting in place excellent policies and programs against bullying. Quite recently some Education Departments have begun to respond, as they should, by insisting that all schools have policies and procedures for dealing with bullying. Resources are becoming available to help schools with the task of educating and training school staff to respond effectively.

The purpose of this handbook is to provide for educators a set of basic facts, ideas and suggested procedures in a convenient format to help eliminate the manifest evil of bullying in schools.

I am encouraged to try my hand at this because over the last 12 years I have kept abreast of bullying research and contributed substantially to it through more than 30 books and papers in international academic research journals. Such research is not very accessible to the general reader, and indeed has needed to be translated, as it were, from the academic jargon into sound practical advice. Although running a school and getting the best out of everyone is a skill that normally develops through personal experience and is honed by practice, we can, I believe, learn from research and benefit from the experience of those who have wrestled with the persistent problem of bullying in schools.

While the main focus of this handbook is on bullying among students, we need to spread the net wider to include the whole school community. It is obvious that bullying and harassment often occur between adults in the workplace. In fact the second wave of research into bullying has centred exclusively on workplace issues. In some schools, teachers have claimed that they are being bullied by their peers, sometimes by students, and occasionally by the parents of students. For their part, students sometimes claim that they are bullied by their teachers. Parents may also believe that teachers have bullied them when they have sought help for their children. Not only are such encounters distressing but also they provide models of inappropriate behaviour that can positively encourage bullying behaviour among students. It is therefore important that in addressing the problem of bullying in schools we should be concerned with the quality of relationships that exist in the whole school community. We need to take this wider perspective.

For the growing number of school educators who want to know what is the research evidence for the judgements that writers make and also wish to go into more detail about specific methods of intervention, I have provided a set of instructive notes and references at the end of this handbook.

2 USING THE HANDBOOK

This handbook is designed primarily for people concerned with the social education of young people, whether as teachers or as parents.

The following are suggestions as to how the handbook may be used.

For school educators

1. First appoint a coordinator for the development of an Anti-Bullying Policy for the school. This person would work with a small number of other staff members to form the Coordinating Committee.

2. Each committee member would then meet with a group of staff to discuss the content of the Handbook. All staff members thus become involved. There can be, if required, several meetings at which the content of the Handbook is discussed. Information from the Appendix can be used to provide overhead transparencies or handouts.

3. At group meetings members should identify ideas and suggestions useful and applicable to their school.

4. At the end of the series of meetings, group leaders should share views expressed by their groups and decide upon what recommendations to make to the School. At this stage the Committee may decide to coopt parent and/or student representation.

5. The Coordinating Committee should then prepare a document for distribution to each staff member outlining proposed actions to counter and reduce bullying.

6. This document may then be discussed at a general Staff Meeting and provide a basis for the school's Anti-Bullying Policy.

For parents

1. Read the Handbook with a view to understanding what ideas and suggestions are **now** being made by educators to reduce bullying.

2. After appraising what is suggested, you will be aware of options that are now available to schools. You will find this useful in understanding what schools and families can do to stop bullying and ensure that any approaches you might make to the school are informed.

3. The Handbook can help parents who are considering educational alternatives and wish to choose the school that best provides for the safety of their children.

WHY BOTHER?

Occasionally – less and less often I am glad to say – you meet somebody who does not see, or does not want to see, what the fuss is about. You may hear these things said:

> *'There may be a few schools around where nasty things like bullying and violence occur, but I'm glad to say that nothing like that happens at my school.'*

> *'Sure kids do bully each other. So what! It helps to toughen them up. Shouldn't wrap them in cotton wool, anyway. No real harm is done.'*

> *'There has always been bullying. There will always be bullying. Just human nature. No point in wasting your time trying to stop it.'*

We now know that **none** of these statements is true.

Hundreds of independent studies have been conducted in many countries including Australia to assess the incidence of bullying in all manner of schools[1] and there has never been a study in any school that has reported that bullying was not taking place.

Again, many studies have examined the question of whether children are affected adversely by being bullied and the answer is a unanimous 'yes'. We can list the areas:

1. **Lowered mental health**[2]: damaged self-esteem; increased anxiety; deepened depression; increased likelihood of suicidal thinking; lowered level of happiness;

2. **Induced social maladjustment**[3]: fear of other children; absenteeism from school[4]; and

3. **Physical un-wellness:** rise in medical ill-health symptoms[5].

What is of particular concern is that serious and sustained bullying in schools can have devastating long-term effects on the health and wellbeing of people when they reach adult years[6].

We should recognise too that although most victims are subdued, some become alienated and bitter, plot revenge and can be extremely dangerous to others[7].

Finally there **are** grounds for optimism. Studies show that there are large variations between schools in the prevalence of peer victimisation[8], and these cannot be accounted for in terms of background characteristics of students and their families. More crucially, interventions to reduce bullying have been shown to work[9].

Understanding Bullying

WHAT IS BULLYING?

How you define and describe bullying is of great practical importance because it determines what you focus upon and ultimately what you do about it.

You need to be clear what it is and what it is not. To do justice to what bullying is, you need to recognise that:

1. **It begins when somebody (or a group of persons) wants to hurt someone or put that person under pressure.**

   Such a desire is a necessary but not sufficient condition for bullying to occur. Remember that a desire to hurt or pressure somebody may not be expressed in hurtful action, in which case bullying may not take place[1].

2. **Bullying involves a desire to hurt + hurtful action.**

   There may be actions of different kinds: physical or verbal or gestural, direct or indirect, or commonly a combination of these. But, in addition, there is an imbalance of power[2], at least in the situation in which the bullying takes place.

3. **Bullying involves a desire to hurt + hurtful action + a power imbalance.**

   Although you may reasonably want to stop it, fighting or quarrelling between people of equal strength or power is not bullying. But in addition, bullying is conceived as behaviour that is not just[3].

4. **Bullying involves a desire to hurt + hurtful action + a power imbalance + an unjust use of power.**

   Hence we must always ask whether the hurtful use of superior power is justified or not (see Section 7). In addition, bullying actions are typically repeated.

5. **Bullying involves a desire to hurt + hurtful action + a power imbalance + an unjust use of power + (typically) repetition[4].**

   It is characteristic of bullying that the perpetrator enjoys the domination[5] that is being demonstrated and the victim feels oppressed[6].

> **Bullying involves a desire to hurt + hurtful action + a power imbalance + (typically) repetition + an unjust use of power + evident enjoyment by the aggressor and a sense of being oppressed on the part of the victim.**

5 GENDER, RACE, DISABILITY AND SOCIAL CLASS

Over the last 10 years or so there has been a lot said and written about bullying and harassment occurring as a consequence of prejudiced thinking and discrimination, more especially on the basis of gender, race and disability. Education Departments have understandably emphasised the importance of these factors[1].

1. **Gender:** How individuals construct 'masculinity' and 'femininity' can have a significant effect on how they treat others. For example, when a boy sees himself as very tough, aggressive or macho, he is prone to despise and harass other boys who are gentle and artistic[2]. Similarly, a girl who sees herself as 'feminine' in the conventional sense may look down on other girls who are rough, 'unladylike' or 'butch'. This line of thinking does indeed explain some bullying behaviour, for instance that of boys who deride and seek to upset those they see as 'gay'. Sex-based harassment has been identified as occurring frequently among Australian schoolchildren[3].

    Most bullying goes on within gender groups. Generally, physical bullying goes on mainly between boys and relational bullying goes on mainly between girls. Verbal bullying, however, is not uncommon between genders, with girls being subjected much more to disparaging and hurtful remarks from boys than vice-versa[4]. The problem of changing the attitudes and verbal behaviour of boys towards girls in schools – and its continuation in later years – is a particularly pressing one.

2. **Race:** Although the term is now seen as having little scientific credibility and is consequently avoided in favour of 'ethnicity', there can be no doubt that feelings of superiority because one belongs to a particular ethnic group, usually a socially dominant group, can give rise to bullying and harassment[5]. At the same time, research has shown that racial or ethnic group differences need not render one group more susceptible to being bullied than another[6].

3. **Disability:** Bullying is sometimes directed towards children who do not have the same physical or mental capabilities as others, for example children who are diagnosed as ADD or have speech defects[7].

4. **Social class:** Where there is a mix of children from families of high and low socioeconomic status, some being rich and others poor or unemployed, the possibility of bullying, especially through social exclusion, must always be present. However, research does not consistently support the view that, in a school, children from families of low socioeconomic status are victimised more than others[8].

Explanations that relate to the above factors can account for a good deal of bullying and harassment, and useful instructive material has become available to schools in recent years. But not all bullying can be explained in this way. And we should bear in mind that there are many examples of schools in which differences in social class and ethnicity do not inevitably give rise to children bullying each other.

6   POWER INEQUALITIES

Differences in power between individuals and between groups make bullying possible.

Power may be defined generally as the capacity to produce an intended effect. It may be used or abused.

In schools there are large differences in power that can be employed to bully others This is partly due to the fact that schools cater for children of different ages, different levels of maturity and different personal and social characteristics. Further, the element of compulsion in school education implies that the staff in a school must have the power to act authoritatively in dealing with students. Added to this, hierarchical structure in school organisations results in some staff members having a higher degree of institutional or legitimate power than others.

We can identify a number of specific sources of power that some members of a school community enjoy:

1. **The capacity to dominate others physically:** This may be related to size, strength[1] and fighting skills. This is likely to be more important among boys, especially in Primary School when physical encounters are more common.

2. **Sharpness of tongue:** Related to verbal skills, especially quickness of wit. As children become older, these qualities become more potent means of bullying others.

3. **Ability to call on others for support:** Related to popularity, social skills and the capacity to manipulate others. This applies especially to so-called relational bullying[2].

4. **Status in a group:** Related to having valued accomplishments, such as sporting ability, being personally attractive, being a member of a majority, mainstream group as opposed, for example, to being in an ethnic minority, disabled or not heterosexual.

5. **Institutionalised or ascribed authority:** Related to position in an organisation, for example principal, teacher or student, prefect and, in some schools, senior as opposed to junior.

Bear in mind that power is not fixed. A person may acquire or lose power. For example, a child may learn to become more assertive; a teacher may lose the capacity to control a class. Power is fluid.

Secondly, note that power is often situation-bound; for example, the capacity to dominate physically may be a means of bullying in the schoolyard but not in a well-run classroom.

WHEN FORCEFULNESS IS NOT BULLYING

It should not be assumed that when a more powerful person acts forcefully in a given situation and places someone under some pressure that he or she is necessarily engaging in bullying. It is acknowledged that persons in authority should have some powers to insist on appropriate behaviour within certain defined areas.

The use of teacher authority with students

Currently teachers are, under some circumstances, empowered to employ verbal reprimands, exclude children from classes or selected activities, and order detentions.

On the other hand, the use of physical force (hitting or caning), the continual use of sarcasm at a child's expense, repeatedly shouting at or threatening children are regarded as unjustified and can be described as 'bullying'.

The line between the forceful use of teacher authority and bullying is sometimes not easy to draw. Indeed, in recent years the 'correct' line has repeatedly shifted[1].

The use of authority consistent with assigned non-teaching role

The role may fit into a school hierarchy, as in Principal, Deputy Principal, other staff, and entail power to direct others. In addition, some roles may have a specialised non-hierarchical function, as in the case of Year Coordinator, Librarian and School Secretary. Each has a degree of authority that may be appropriately applied. For example, a principal may allocate staff duties; a librarian may insist on quiet in the library. Bullying occurs when such authority is misapplied or used excessively.

Roles may also be assigned among students, as occurs when prefects or school captains are elected or appointed. Again, bullying can occur when such leaders act in ways that are not consistent with role requirements. This is evident in schools where senior students are empowered to discipline junior students and sometimes engage in victimisation. This can happen to a greater degree in Boarding Schools.

Degree of provocation

Sometimes when force is used by a more powerful person, it is in response to provocation by an individual or group; for example, when junior students set out to tease older students or when teachers are targeted and class work disrupted by mischievous students. Although the circumstances may not fully justify a forceful reaction, they may reduce the culpability of the actions and should be judged accordingly.

We may conclude that although in most cases it is not difficult to recognise what is bullying, there are certainly grey areas. What should be done in these circumstances must be continually debated.

8 THE MEANS OF BULLYING

The ways people bully can be classified (with examples) as follows.

	DIRECT	INDIRECT
Verbal abuse	Verbal insults Unfair criticism Name calling	Persuading another person to criticise or insult someone Spreading malicious rumours Anonymous phone calls and emails
Gestural abuse	Threatening or obscene gestures Menacing stares	Deliberate turning away or averting one's gaze to ignore someone
Physical means	Striking Throwing things Using a weapon Removing and hiding belongings	Getting another person to assault someone
Relational bullying	Forming coalitions against someone	Persuading people to exclude someone

For all groups of persons – students, teachers and parents – **verbal means** are the most common form of bullying. The means may vary in sophistication or subtlety, from crude name-calling and up-front insults, more common among children, to the use of cruel sarcasm, innuendo and rational-sounding (but knowingly unfair) criticism employed by older students and adults. **Indirect verbal bullying** may occur when the perpetrator seeks to hurt someone without revealing his or her identity. **Gestural bullying** again may vary in subtlety from finger signs and tongue poking to rolling of the eyes and a deliberately inappropriate poker face. In most school communities **physical means** are the least commonly practised, but occur more frequently among boys and among younger students. Although not physically hurtful, the continual removing of belongings is common in many schools. **Relational bullying** depends for its effectiveness on deliberately reducing the enjoyment a victim may have through satisfying personal relationships, and appears to be practised more among girls.

A further distinction is between bullying perpetrated by **individuals** and bullying by **groups**. The distinction is sometimes difficult to make because individual bullies are often sustained by groups or associates. But some bullying is exclusively one to one, and some essentially a group against an individual who may be a student, a teacher or a parent.

In practice, bullying may involve several or all of these means, but remember that it is not just the actions themselves that constitute bullying. One must also take into account the power imbalance and whether the actions were justified or not.

9 SEXUAL HARASSMENT

Sexual harassment is akin to bullying and should be included when a school considers what it can do to stop bullying[1].

It may be defined as unwelcome conduct targeting the gender of another person that may reasonably be judged as offensive, humiliating or intimidating.

Thus whilst the first and essential criterion is whether the conduct of the perpetrator is unwelcome, a further consideration is the judgement of a fully informed and reasonable person.

Broadly, sexual harassment implies that a person is being put under unacceptable pressure in the area of their sexuality and accordingly feels oppressed. The perpetrator or perpetrators, as in bullying, are abusing their power.

We should bear in mind that sexual harassment can and does take place from time to time between people of the same gender as well as between males and females[2]. It can happen between schoolchildren of all ages, between staff members and between staff and students.

As in bullying, we recognise different means by which sexual harassment is carried out. These can include:

1. **Physical means:** as in unwanted contact of a sexual nature, for example touching breasts or genitalia.

2. **Verbal:** as in unwanted comments, which may be spoken or written, drawing attention to a person's actual or alleged sexual characteristics or sexual orientation, such as having big, small or 'no' breasts; being heterosexual, homosexual or 'non-sexual'. Comments or written messages, for example by email, may suggest that a person lacks an acceptable sexual identity, being, for example, 'cold', 'frigid' or 'butch'.

3. **Gestural:** as in offensive finger gestures, cynically thrown 'kisses' or deliberate staring intended to embarrass.

4. **Indirect:** as in spreading rumours orally or through graffiti about someone's sexual activities or orientation and seeking to have others treat that person deprecatingly because of their sexuality.

The motivation behind sexual harassment is commonly to hurt in some way, which is invariably the case with bullying. But one must bear in mind that in some cases what is experienced by the victim as sexual harassment is a crude and socially unacceptable attempt to gain sexual satisfaction or even to initiate or advance a sexual relationship with someone. Hence, there is sometimes a need to distinguish between sexual harassment and bullying.

10) BULLYING AS A DYNAMIC PROCESS

It's useful to see bullying as a process that typically persists over time with outcomes depending on a number of definable factors.

To understand how bullying begins, start with a scenario in which someone is seen as a potential victim of systematic aggressive behaviour.

Anybody may fit this category, but it is more likely that the potential victim will display characteristics that suggest weakness and vulnerability[1].

Bullying is deliberate. Plans are made to put the targeted person under pressure, typically to hurt, undermine and humiliate.

Action of different kinds follows and the cycle begins, sometimes with other people joining in to maintain the bullying.

BULLYING CYCLE BEGINS

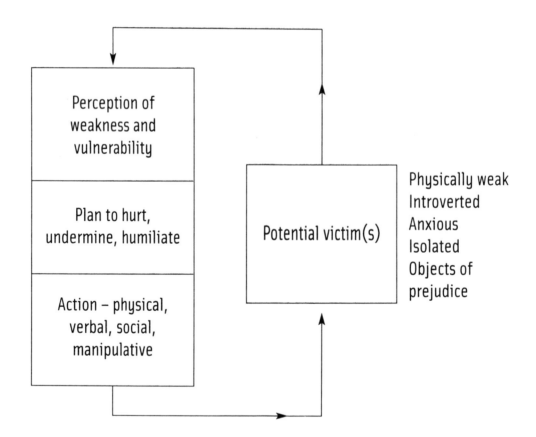

11 THE PASSIVE VICTIM

Some victims may be called passive victims. They do not resist. The following diagram shows what typically happens.

BULLYING AND THE PASSIVE VICTIM

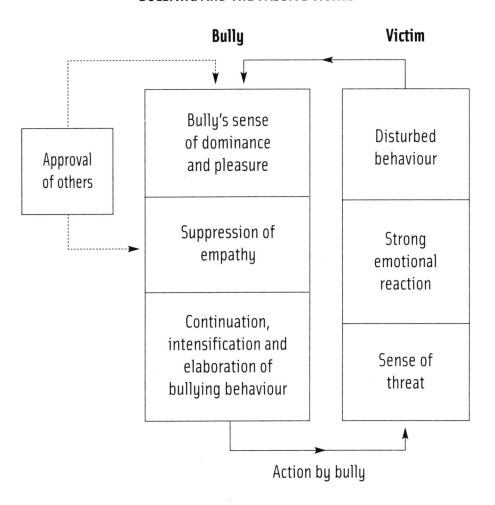

The reaction of the passive victim is typically one of fear, either because the threat is overwhelming or because of a fearful disposition, or both. The victim may be petrified.

He or she may see no way of responding effectively. During the bullying, the victim may appear zombie-like or alternatively wildly emotional. Subsequently, the victim is likely to appear upset and depressed.

The victim's reaction may reinforce the bully's or bullies' behaviour. They have achieved the intended effect. If there is approval from others – especially from by-standers when the bullying occurs – the sense of dominance and pleasure may increase[1]. The chances of an empathic reaction to the victim's distress are lessened. The bullying is likely to continue. It may become more elaborate as new ways of bullying the victim are discovered. It may become more intense. As long as the bullying gives satsfaction and there is no intervention the cycle continues. We know that such cycles can continue unabated for many weeks, months, even years[2].

12 / THE RESISTANT VICTIM

With the resistant victim a different story may unfold. In this case the victim may see the bullying behaviour as a challenge rather than a foregone conclusion and make plans to counter it in some way. The diagram suggests different possibilities.

BULLYING AND THE RESISTANT VICTIM

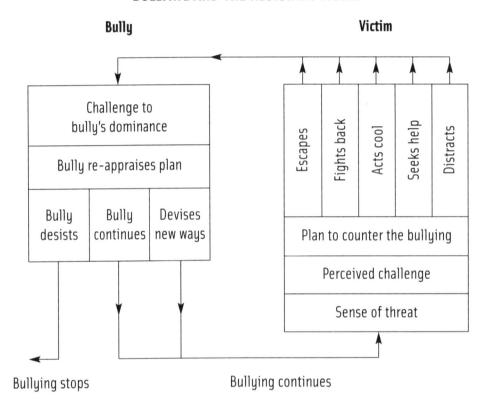

The victim may seek to employ one or more of these ways of coping:

1. **Escapes:** The victim may find ways of escaping from the bullying situation and may minimise chances of encountering the bully/bullies on future occasions.

2. **Fights back:** Fighting back, physically or verbally, may be an option. In some circumstances a student may overcome the problem by taking appropriate physical training or (less dangerously) learning how to react more assertively.

3. **Acts cool:** Appearing unperturbed, acting nonchalant, may sometimes be the best way to respond, especially with low level teasing or name-calling.

4. **Seeks help:** Help may be sought from various quarters; from other students, parents, and school authorities. Many students are unwilling to seek help because 'dobbing' is unacceptable by peers or because it may make matters worse[1].

5. **Distracts[2]:** Distracting, amusing or placating a bully so that he or she begins to behave more positively is a possible strategy.

Under some circumstances each of these strategies may be effective in lessening or countering the bullying. But often these strategies are unsuccssful and the bullying continues.

WHY SOME PEOPLE BULLY

As we have seen, the existence of power imbalances in a school community make bullying possible. Of course, not all people make use of their greater power to bully someone. Here are suggestions as to why some do.

1. **They think that bullying pays;** in some schools they are admired by others; they are able to get what they want; and they are less likely than others to be victimised[1].

2. **They are aggressive and impulsive,** which makes them constitutionally more inclined to engage in bullying.

3. **They enjoy the submission of others**[2].

4. **Bullying others is consistent with a macho or imposing image** a person may have, especially if one is male[3] but increasingly so for females.

5. **It seems like fun**[4], especially when one is part of a group engaged in teasing someone.

6. **They have relatively low levels of empathy,** which results in a bully being unaffected by the evident distress of others[5].

7. **Prejudice leads them to believe that some kinds of people deserve to be bullied;** for example, people of a different ethnic group or of a different sexual orientation.

8. **A generalised hostility towards others** has been engendered by negative experiences with parents and families, especially feeling unloved and/or over-controlled[6].

9. **They have been influenced by aggressive 'models',** in real life and/or by viewing violent videos[7].

10. **The victim is perceived as having provoked the negative treatment;** commonly bullies see their bullying behaviour as 'pay-backs'[8].

11. **Chronic boredom at school** may result in bullying as a means of making life more interesting.

12. **The achievement of desired goals** is seen as more important than the insensitive means employed to attain them. This applies particularly to some people in management positions[9].

13. **They are slaves to authority** prepared unquestioningly to do their bosses' 'dirty work' by imposing on others[10].

14. **They see it as part of their role;** for example, as a prefect or teacher[11].

Some of these proposed explanations for bullying behaviour relate to personality, others to the social context or to social and societal influences. Each may contribute.

14 WHY SOME PEOPLE DO NOT BULLY

Since a primary aim in countering bullying is to prevent it from happening at all, it is sensible to ask the question: Why is it that some students do not bully, or do so very rarely?

The most obvious reason might be because in general they can't, being less powerful than other students. This is true of some. However, there are numerous cases of students who believe they are more able than others to bully their peers if they wanted to, but do not do so[1]. They do not bully because:

1. **They feel that bullying is wrong.** Substantial numbers of students report that they 'would feel ashamed of themselves' if they bullied someone[2].

2. **They have a high level of empathy** and dislike to see people suffer.

3. **They have social skills**[3] that enable them to get what they want without resorting to bullying.

4. **They are generally so occupied** and enjoying what they are doing that bullying someone doesn't occur to them or is uninteresting.

5. **They feel they are successful** in what they do at school and not inclined to displace anger or frustration by bullying others.

6. **They see the role they fill as being inconsistent with undermining others;** for example, as a prefect, football captain, peer support member or even a 'good student'.

7. **They have been exposed repeatedly to positive modelling** by influential peers or adults.

8. **They believe that bullying others doesn't pay.** This may be because they believe that negative consequences will follow if they do engage in acts of bullying (for instance, they believe that school authorities will find out and impose sanctions); and their bullying will be deplored (not admired) by those who matter to them (friends, parents, possibly teachers).

9. **They have enjoyed positive experiences in the home** and generally feel positive towards others.

10. **They have internalised moral principles** that are incompatible with bullying.

11. **They feel obliged to accept the rules of the school** which indicate that bullying behaviour is not acceptable.

Action to Counter Bullying

15 SETTING GOALS

It is sensible to begin by setting out what you hope to achieve through an anti-bullying program for your school.

Here are my suggestions:

> **The general aim of the program is to make the school a safer, happier place for everyone.**

Progress to this goal is indicated by:

1. A reduction in the number of persons who are victimised by others.

2. A reduction in the severity of victimisation.

3. A reduction in the number of people who engage in bullying others.

4. An increase in the support that is provided to those who are victimised in any way.

You need to consider ways in which progress towards these goals can be assessed. The following are some suggestions:

1. Make use of anonymous questionnaires from which reliable and relevant self-report data can be obtained. (Section 19 describes available questionnaire resources.)

2. Make assessments before the anti-bullying program is put into effect and again some time afterwards. Allow at least a one-year interval between testing[1]. Remember that a program may actually raise awareness of what constitutes bullying, and that if there is a significant reduction in reported victimisation, this probably underestimates the actual reduction.

3. In your analysis of the data, identify precisely where and in what ways changes have occurred, for example according to year and gender and in relation to both behaviour and attitudes. You may also wish to assess whether there have been changes in behaviour and attitudes towards specific groups, such as ethnic minorities.

4. Gauge whether the help provided to victimised students has really been effective in helping them to cope.

5. One focus should be on how students who have engaged in repeated bullying have changed (if at all) as a result of school disciplinary activities and/or counselling.

6. Gather supplementary data based on judgements from students and teachers who were present at school before and after the intervention.

7. Because a program may have many elements, it is useful to seek to identify which elements were responsible for any change.

MAKING A PLAN

Here is a plan that may be adopted (or adapted) to reduce bullying in one's school.

1. **Educate the school community about bullying.** This is a necessary first step and implies both an understanding of the phenomena of bullying and a knowledge of what can be done to reduce its occurrence. The educational process should include in different ways and to a different extent the school staff, students and parents.

2. **Find out what is happening between members of the school community that is relevant to bullying.** You need to understand the nature and scope of the problem before it can be effectively addressed.

3. **Develop an appropriate and well supported Anti-Bullying Policy.** This should be based upon the school's understanding of bullying and especially what has been discovered about bullying at your school. It should provide a guide as to what is to be done.

4. **Establish what staff can do in their everyday work to reduce bullying and support students who are being victimised at school.** What can be done should be communicated to all staff members and serve as a guide and reminder of how they can help ease the problem.

5. **Ensure that teachers talk with students about bullying.** Provide guidance to teachers on how this can be done in such a way as to discourage bullying and gain student cooperation in countering peer victimisation.

6. **Empower students.** Create opportunities and provide necessary support or training for students to play a positive role in countering bullying and improving peer relations in the school.

7. **Devise procedures for dealing appropriately with incidents of bullying.** Alternative approaches need to be considered and evaluated, and distinctions made according to the nature and severity of the bullying.

8. **Provide support for those who are victimised.** Guidelines are needed on the role staff may play in helping students involved in bully/victim problems and how help can best be provided.

9. **Work cooperatively with parents.** This includes setting out how parents can be included in plans to reduce bullying, and how the school can work most effectively with parents whose children become involved in problems at school as victims or as bullies.

17 EDUCATING THE SCHOOL COMMUNITY

Knowledge of bullying in schools and its effects on children varies widely from school to school and also between members of the school community. Before an effective response to the problem can be made, a good knowledge base is needed by those who devise plans to stop bullying and all those whose cooperation is needed to carry out the plans: students and parents as well as staff.

Education of school staff: Teacher education about bullying has increased markedly in recent years, largely through in-service seminars and workshops, and also through the growing availability of helpful resources on the subject. Nevertheless, schools need to keep up to date on relevant information and methods. Finding out about what is happening in the relations between students is a vital part of the process (see Sections 18 and 19). In addition, it is extremely desirable for schools to acquire or access the best resources now available – books, articles, relevant internet sites and videos. A short list of recommended resources is provided for you[1].

Staff seminars and study groups: These are valuable for staff members to share and discuss what has been learned. In particular, a Queensland Education Department video[2] can be used to focus staff discussion on different kinds of bullying encountered in schools. There are also useful videos for schools examining how students can help counter bullying through peer mediation or, more directly, as peer counsellors[3]. It is often useful to invite expert speakers to inform and lead discussions and to explore methods of preventing bullying and dealing with problems.

Education for students: This can and should be provided by teachers in classrooms and, where possible, be part of curriculum content (see Section 23). Again there are some excellent resources that should ideally be acquired. Some of these provide help in planning lessons or discussions about bullying[4]. There are also videos that can be shown to students to raise awareness of the problem and stimulate discussion[5]. Good advice is now available through the Internet on coping with bullying[6]. There are also books that provide advice on how students can learn to cope more effectively with bullying[7]. Make sure that students are told about Safety Houses[8]. Ensure that there are relevant books on bullying in the school library.

Education for parents about bullying: This is vital. Schools should seek to involve parents in the plans they make to counter bullying, hold meetings with parents to discuss the issue, keep them informed (for example, through newsletters) about bullying and about their rights as parents if their child is bullied (see Sections 32 and 34), as well as about how they can collaborate with the school. Some books have been written to help parents and families if a family member is being bullied at school[9]. Advice for parents is also available through the Internet[10].

Further information about bullying: The Australian Council for Educational Research (ACER) is an important source of information about bullying in schools. They carry many resources on this subject and are continually updating both books and videos[11].

18 WHAT IT IS USEFUL TO KNOW ABOUT YOUR SCHOOL

It is useful to know the nature, extent and consequences of bullying in your school in order to:

1. Raise everyone's awareness of the problem to a common level;

2. Motivate everyone to do something to stop the bad things that are happening; and

3. Establish a base-line for subsequent evaluations.

In addition, I think it is useful to know what people (staff, students and parents) would like to see done to counter bullying. This can provide a basis for discussion and drawing up acceptable and well supported plans and procedures.

Answers to these questions have been found to be of particular interest to schools:

◆ What kinds of bullying occur, and how common is each kind?

◆ Where at school does bullying happen most frequently?

◆ What proportion of children are being bullied?

◆ To what extent are different forms of bullying occurring, for example physical, verbal or relational?

◆ In which years or classes is bullying experienced most often?

◆ Are boys and girls bullied in similar or different ways?

◆ What evidence is there of sexual harassment?

◆ Are some groups (for instance, ethnic minority groups) being victimised more than others?

◆ How do students react to being bullied? Do they fight back? Do they tell?

◆ How do students say they have been affected by bullying?

◆ What proportion of children have stayed away from school because of bullying?

◆ How effectively are victimised children being helped?

◆ Do students want to talk about bullying in a classroom discussion?

◆ Are students interested in helping to stop bullying? If so, what might they do?

◆ Do teachers and parents want the school to have an Anti-Bullying Policy?

◆ How do teachers and parents think that cases of bullying should be dealt with?

In addition to these, consider other questions you may want to see answered – questions that may be of particular interest to your school.

19 | HOW TO GET THE FACTS

Much can be gleaned from everyday observations of how students interact with each other in classrooms and playgrounds, how staff treat each other, and the quality of their interactions with students and with parents.

However, given the diversity of impressions observers commonly receive, it is sensible to make use of anonymous[1] questionnaires answered by all the parties: students, teachers and parents.

Fortunately there are several reliable survey instruments that have been widely used in Australia and overseas. (See: http://www.education.unisa.edu.au/bullying/)

They include the following:

The Peer Relations Questionnaire (PRQ) devised by Rigby and Slee (1993). This is a questionnaire for students. It has been used by over 100 schools, providing information about bullying in Primary and Secondary Schools from over 38000 students. It is a comprehensive research instrument that takes approximately 30 minutes to administer. The results need to be analysed by computer.

The Peer Relations Assessment Questionnaires (PRAQs) developed more recently by Rigby (1995). These consist of three versions to be answered by students, teachers and parents respectively. These have also been employed by over 100 schools. They are relatively short and normally take not more than 15 minutes to answer. Tally and summarising sheets are provided to enable the school to summarise the results. It is strongly advised that every staff member takes part in reading a sample of what the respondents say. Opportunity is provided on the questionnaires for respondents to make statements as well as tick optional answers. The PRAQs can help greatly in raising awareness of the nature of the problem and how it is viewed by students, parents and teachers.

The School Relations Assessment Package (SRAP). This new computerised system accessed through the Internet was designed by Rigby and Barnes (2000). Based in part on previous questionnaires but with added content, this resource is available to schools with appropriate computing facilities. On completion of the questionnaires, a summary of group results can be provided within minutes.

For additional information on the questionnaires and the PRQ Manual (Rigby 1997c) contact Dr Barrington Thomas, P.O. Box 104, Point Lonsdale, Victoria, Australia 3225, ph. 03 5258 2340 or fax 08 5258 3878; email: profread@pipeline.com.au

Information on the SRAP is available from Dr K Rigby,
email: ken.rigby@unisa.edu.au
phone: 08 8302 6945 or
Dr A Barnes: alan.barnes@unisa.edu.au
phone: 08 8302 4543.

20 DEVELOPING AN ANTI-BULLYING POLICY

Most schools now agree that they should have a specific Anti-Bullying Policy. This is not the same thing as a School Discipline Policy or a Behaviour Management Policy. It may relate to these, but it needs to take into account the unique features of school bullying as defined earlier and also the perceptions and judgments of members of the school community.

Its purpose is to articulate where the school stands on the issue of bullying and, in general terms, what the school intends to do about it.

These steps are suggested:

1. Hold a meeting with the school staff at which there is a presentation of what has been discovered about bullying at the school from the results of the questionnaires that have been administered. Make sure that the results are succinctly presented and clearly pertinent. It is useful to have a summary of the most relevant results available to every staff member. As well as quantitative information, it is useful to make use of selected quotations from what respondents have written.

2. Make appropriate use of information provided by staff members and parents as well as from students.

3. Discuss the implications from the findings and highlight the need to have a whole-school well coordinated response to the problem.

4. Have the task of formulating a draft Anti-Bullying Policy for the school delegated to a selected group. (See Section 2, Using the Handbook, for suggestions on how the committee might proceed.) This group should be empowered to coopt student and parent representatives.

5. Ensure that the draft policy is critically examined by all interested parties and, if necessary, revised accordingly. To be most effective, the policy must be widely supported by students, teachers and parents.

Bear in mind that an anti-bullying policy should be a response to a situation identified as occurring at a particular school and should reflect the views of that school community. At the same time, it can be helpful to examine and discuss policies that have been produced at other schools and consider how relevant (or irrelevant) they are to one's own school. Examples of school policies to counter bullying are available[1].

WHAT GOES INTO THE POLICY

An Anti-Bullying Policy is a generalised response to bullying. It should provide principles and guidelines, not detailed procedures to deal with every conceivable case. The school will on occasions need flexibility. Here are some suggestions about what such a policy may contain:

1. A strong statement of the school's stand against bullying.

2. A succinct definition of bullying, with illustrations (see Sections 4 and 7).

3. A declaration of the rights of individuals in the school community – students, teachers, other workers and parents – to be free of bullying and (if bullied) to be provided with help and support.

4. A statement of the responsibilities of members of the school community: to abstain personally from bullying others in any way; to actively discourage bullying when it occurs; and to give support to those who are victimised.

5. A general description of what the school will do to deal with incidents of bullying. For example, the severity and seriousness of the bullying will be assessed and appropriate action taken. This may include the use of counselling practices, the imposition of sanctions, interviews with parents and, in extreme cases, suspension from school.

6. An undertaking to evaluate the policy in the near and specified future.

If there are concerns about anything contained in the document, make sure that these are thoroughly examined and resolved. The policy should eventually be widely disseminated, so that everyone in the school community knows what it contains. If necessary, there should be versions for parents of non-English speaking background. Different versions of the policy may be seen as appropriate, for example:

(i) A general policy document consisting of a series of short statements on how the school is responding to the issue of bullying;

(ii) A document for parents explaining what they can do if their child becomes involved in a victim/bully problem at school (see Section 32);

(iii) A document for students on their rights and responsibilities and what they can do if they are victimised or if they see someone else being victimised;

(iv) A document for school staff detailing practical steps they can take when cases of bullying come to their attention. Also, what they can do if they are bullied by anyone at school. This document can include agreed, relevant administrative procedures for dealing with problems and the names of individual staff members who may have been assigned specialised roles for dealing with cases of bullying.

22 WHAT TEACHERS CAN DO ABOUT BULLYING

1. HELPING TO CREATE A SOCIAL ETHOS IN WHICH BULLYING IS LESS LIKELY TO HAPPEN

(i) Personally modelling pro-social, respectful behaviour in interactions with students, parents and other staff.

(ii) Developing and maintaining good classroom management[1]. Avoiding unduly pressuring or bullying students. (Sometimes teachers under stress go beyond being appropriately authoritative and descend into sarcasm and intimidation.)

(iii) Ensuring as far as possible that the educational tasks and the way they are presented engage the interests of all students. (Sometimes students bully out of boredom.)

(iv) Where practicable, include tasks that require cooperation between class members for successful completion[2].

(v) Minimise situations in which students are unoccupied, unsupervised, and in close proximity to others whom they may not wish to be near, especially over extended periods. This can and often does occur when teachers are late for a class or called away from a class, or when students are waiting for long periods for a canteen to open or for public transport to arrive, or are in transit on long journeys by bus.

2. ACTIVELY DISCOURAGING BULLYING

(i) By being observant and responding appropriately when bullying occurs in classrooms or at recess, according to the nature and severity of the bullying (see Sections 27 and 28).

(ii) Where appropriate, informing other staff members of incidents and initiating procedures agreed upon by the school to deal with perpetrators.

3. PROVIDING SUPPORT AND ADVICE

(i) By being open to listen to students who believe that they are being victimised (and to their parents) if they wish to talk about it.

(ii) By offering advice or suggestions, when asked, or by providing access to specialised counselling help if needed (see Section 30).

4. EDUCATING ABOUT BULLYING

(i) By facilitating class discussions on bullying at school.

(ii) Where practicable, developing in students relevant skills in assertiveness, conflict resolution and peer mediation (see Section 26).

23 TALKING WITH STUDENTS IN CLASS ABOUT BULLYING

Getting the active cooperation of students is a vital part of countering bullying. This involves talking with students individually and in groups about bullying and how they can help to stop it. It is more easily done with Primary School children and late Secondary School students[1]. But in all years, many students are keen to talk about it and comparatively few are against doing so. Students nearly always dislike and despise bullies and can, with your help, assist greatly in developing and implementing school policy. Here are some suggestions for conducting class discussions:

1. Be clear about what you want to achieve with the group. For example:

    (i)   recognise what bullying is;

    (ii) experience feelings of concern and empathy for victims;

    (iii) make constructive suggestions about what can be done to stop bullying; and

    (iv) undertake to act in ways to discourage bullying.

2. Work with the class using methods that are suitable for the age group and with which _you_ are comfortable. But avoid a threatening, authoritarian approach which will antagonise some and polarise attitudes in the group. Don't preach. Better to treat the class members as a resource for dealing with the problem. Here are some ideas:

    (i)   **Arouse interest in the topic of bullying by first viewing an interesting video or film on the subject,** reading a book, examining relevant newspaper reports, or conducting a role-play illustrating bullying[2], or by having students write an essay describing conflicts between students at school. A focused discussion of bullying can then follow, leading to an examination of what can be done about it and, possibly, resolutions agreed on by the class.

    (ii) **Present specific problems relating to bullying incidents;** for example, how bystanders can be motivated to help rather than hinder students who are being targeted as victims.

    (iii) **Invite those who are interested in doing something to stop bullying to form an Anti-Bullying Committee,** run by an interested teacher who is prepared to listen to their ideas about what students can do to reduce bullying in their school (see Section 24).

In addition, discuss with other teachers ways in which classes can be motivated to help reduce bullying. Be prepared to share both successes and failures.

ROLES FOR EMPOWERED STUDENTS

In recent years there has been much attention given to the part that students can actively play in reducing bullying. There are some clear advantages in gaining their assistance. We should bear in mind:

1. Students are much more likely to go to other students for help than to go to teachers when they are bullied.

2. Students usually have a much better, more realistic understanding of the nature of the relationships students have with each other.

3. Students are usually around when bullying takes place, especially during school breaks and to and from school; teachers are rarely present at these times.

4. Some students are strongly motivated to help resolve interpersonal conflicts and can demonstrate high level skills in mediation and conflict resolution.

5. Students can often provide much needed information on bully/victim problems. They can coordinate their activities with those of staff members to discourage bullying.

THE ANTI-BULLYING COMMITTEE

This concept has been successfully employed in a number of schools in Australia[1].

1. It is composed of students who have volunteered to work together under the leadership of a staff member to help reduce bullying in a school.

2. Ideally it has students from every year of school and – in coeducational schools – has an appropriate gender balance.

3. It may include students who in the past have engaged in bullying, provided they have clearly committed themselves to helping to stop bullying.

4. The role of the staff member leading the group is to provide a sounding board for student ideas on how bullying at school can be countered, to encourage constructive plans and to provide the link between school policies and student initiatives.

Some of the things students may do are given on the next page.

Note: If students are to take on special roles, these should be defined clearly and unambiguously so that students know the limits of their responsibilities. They must also be provided with suitable training and support (see Section 26).

25 WHAT STUDENTS CAN DO

These are suggestions as to what students can do:

1. **Participate in the development of the school policy against bullying.** Student representatives can make useful contributions and help to evaluate suggestions.

2. **Speak up at school assemblies against bullying.** Students speaking up against bullying is often far more influential than speeches made by staff members.

3. **Form a welcoming committee** for new students when they start school.

4. **Help in the development of an orientation package for new students.**

5. **Visit feeder schools to reassure students** who will be coming to their school that they can count on being helped if they encounter any troublesome students.

6. **Help in publicising anti-bullying policies** by designing posters and writing about bullying in school magazines.

7. **Make it known that they will help fellow students** who have problems related to bullying. Students may be informed about how particular student-helpers can be contacted.

8. **Give advice to students** on how they might handle conflict constructively, avoid being bullied and get help if needed.

9. **Look out for students** who are having problems in their relations with others and offer them support.

10. **Provide staff with information** about ongoing bully/victim problems, for example, where problems may be arising, and which students are involved.

11. **Help directly in the resolution of bully/victim problems**[1]. Depending on the readiness of the school to approve the involvement of students in counselling or dispute resolution roles, selected students may act to resolve bully/victim problems under the general supervision of a staff member. For such work the school may decide to provide special training and access appropriate resources (see Section 26).

12. **Help monitor changes in student behaviour** as a consequence of anti-bullying initiatives.

26 ACCESSING USEFUL RESOURCES

There are now abundant resources aimed at reducing conflict in schools. These are relevant to addressing bullying because they help to create a school environment in which people enjoy more constructive relationships and are able to settle disputes that may otherwise end up in one person bullying another. Schools may decide to access or acquire some of these resources as a means to producing a happier, more peaceable school in which bullying is much less likely to happen.

Peer Support is one such resource. This is a service available in most States[1]. It is concerned with fostering the physical and mental wellbeing of young people through the help they can receive from other students who have been suitably trained. There is a two-stage process: a Peer Support organisation first trains the teachers in the required methodology, then teachers train the students. Sessions are timetabled for senior students to work with groups of junior students, addressing relevant issues and suggesting solutions to problems. Anti-bullying is one of the issues that receives attention.

Conflict Resolution Skills are the means by which disputes may be resolved without the use of force or through the compliance of the less powerful party. Several useful publications have provided detailed descriptions of them and explained their value[2]. More recently, drama and role-play have been used to develop insights and teach methods relevant to resolving conflicts at school[3]. If these skills are well taught, bullying resulting from unresolved disputes will become less likely. Also students acquiring these skills become more adept at handling difficult interpersonal relations, including attempts at bullying them. They may also become better at helping others in such situations.

Mediation: This focuses on how a third party can help people engaged in a dispute or conflict that they are unable to resolve. Teachers who wish to acquire relevant skills can do so by enrolling in centres of tertiary education[4]. How effectively they can employ such skills in resolving student conflicts including bully/victim problems depends in part on the extent to which students trust them to undertake this task.

In some States, training is now available from professionals who provide workshops and seminars for students and also for teachers who subsequently oversee and monitor the students' work[5]. Generally, peer mediation practised by students does not extend to cases where serious cases of bullying occur (these normally require adult intervention), but mediation by students in other cases may help to promote a school ethos in which bullying cannot flourish. Whether senior students may (and should) be trained to deal with bully/victim cases is controversial. Schools may, however, wish to investigate the feasibility of students engaging in this work.

Schools deciding to employ resources and methods described above should first count the cost (in time and expense) and also understand that a strong, sustained commitment to the practices is needed if their use is to be effective.

27 BULLY/VICTIM CASES

No two cases are exactly the same but we can identify broad types of cases and these can have implications for how you go about trying to solve them.

THE INDIVIDUAL BULLY[1]

1. The bullying is occurring in an ongoing relationship or derives from a past relationship. It is sustained by an unresolved dispute between two people. You may decide that mediation could work.

2. The bully is picking on one victim after another. This is the serial bully[2]. Action generally needs to be taken by the school authorities to ensure that such behaviour is monitored and negatively reinforced, and alternative pro-social behaviours encouraged.

3. A very dominant person in authority may seriously bully an entire group[3]. Work is needed with such a person to examine alternative means of influencing others and, in extreme cases, removal from the situation where people are being harmed.

BULLYING BY GROUPS

1. The group may consist of a duo who strongly reinforce each other in their acts of bullying[4]. They seek victims. Sometimes one is clearly the leader and the other the accomplice. The duo can sometimes be extremely dangerous and their activities must be taken very seriously.

2. The group may be composed of members of roughly equal power and have relatively high cohesiveness; sometimes they have a ringleader. They may enjoy tormenting individuals with little or no justification because of a shared pleasure in doing so[5]. Sometimes the target of bullying by the class is the teacher[6].

3. The group may be non-cohesive and include virtually everyone in an organisation. The bullying behaviour is directed towards an 'outsider' and may become automatic for everyone[7].

4. Sometimes dominant groups bully other groups. This can occur when groups differ in power and status, the more powerful 'in-group' acting abusively towards another group or groups[8].

It is often best in cases of group bullying to work with group members individually (as in the Method of Shared Concern, see Section 29). However, if the group is brought together to confront the problem it is best to include a number of pro-social students who can influence the outcome (see the so-called 'No Blame Approach', Section 29).

28 ASSESSING SEVERITY

As well as the type of case, you need to take into account the severity of the bullying. It is unreasonable to treat thoughtless (though hurtful) teasing in the same way as continual physical assault. The following diagram suggests how bullying is generally distributed in a school.

SEVERITY OF BULLYING BEHAVIOUR

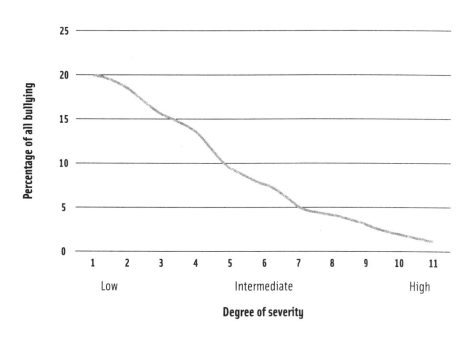

The figure shows the approximate distribution of bullying behaviour according to severity. To estimate severity one would need to take into account:

(i) **the nature of the action,** for example mild teasing which is generally not experienced as very hurtful, versus physical assault which is normally much more devastating;

(ii) **the frequency of bullying acts,** for example whether daily, weekly or less often; and

(iii) **the duration of the bullying,** whether over a short or long time period.

For some purposes, for example in providing protection or support to victims, one may wish to take into account the vulnerability of the individual being targeted.

Low severity commonly involves thoughtless periodic teasing, name-calling and occasional exclusion. This can be annoying and unpleasant and can escalate and then involve more serious forms of bullying. Most bullying is at this level.

An intermediate level of bullying occurs when a child is subjected for a time to forms of harassment that are both systematic and hurtful. These may include cruel teasing, continual exclusion and some threats or some relatively mild physical abuse, for example pushing or tripping.

Severe bullying occurs when the harassment is cruel and intense, especially if it occurs over an extended period and is very distressing to the victim. It often involves serious physical assaults, but can still be severe when it is non-physical if the methods used are unremitting, occur over an extended period and are psychologically damaging.

ALTERNATIVE TREATMENTS

To some extent the appropriate treatment of bully/victim problems can be linked to their degree of severity. But you should also bear in mind that different types of cases may require different approaches (see Section 13). These are guidelines only.

LOW SEVERITY

These cases should **never** be ignored.

Talk with the bully or bullies pointing out the evident distress felt by the victim; explain the inappropriateness or unacceptability to the school of the teasing or name-calling; and (where possible) encourage and reinforce pro-social ways of responding on the part of the bully.

Talk with the victim to discover whether he or she has in any way provoked the bullying behaviour. Suggest ways in which the victim may be able to deal with the situation and access resources, for example friends who might help.

Undertake to monitor carefully what happens next and be prepared to intervene (see Intermediate level) if the situation deteriorates.

INTERMEDIATE LEVEL

Alternative approaches have been suggested. In developing its school policy, the school must decide which approaches it will endorse. These include:

The No Blame Approach[1]: This can apply when a group of students is involved. Once identified, the victim is interviewed and asked to describe what has been happening and how he or she has been feeling about it. A group of students is convened, including the bullies, as well as other children expected to propose constructive solutions. The problem and the victim's reactions to the ill-treatment are described to them. They are left to come up with and implement an agreed solution. This approach has been used effectively in Primary Schools and in some Secondary Schools.

The Method of Shared Concern[2]: With this method the bullies are seen individually. The interviewer shares his or her concern for what has been happening to the victim, and invites the bully to take responsible action to remedy the situation. Further work with the victim and the bullies as a group follow so as to effect a true reconciliation. Importantly, developments are carefully monitored. In a large majority of cases the method is effective.

The application of appropriate consequences[3]: This is a more traditional approach which seeks to ascertain the degree of blame attributable to the bullies and then to provide 'consequences'; that is, non-physical sanctions to deter further bullying.

HIGH SEVERITY

This typically requires a careful inquiry into precisely what has happened, conducting interviews with the bullies, victims and observers. Serious talks are conducted with the parents of the bullies. Sanctions may be applied, including possible suspension of the perpetrators. In extreme cases there may be police involvement, possibly charges laid. In some States there is the possibility of a resolution of the problem through the use of **Community Counselling**[4].

> **Note:** The methods of intervention described above should be examined in more detail and thoroughly discussed before they are applied (see notes 1–4 for this Section). Schools need to develop clear procedures, and may assign special roles for staff carrying out such interventions in accordance with school policy (see Section 21).

30 HELPING THE VICTIMS

One of the responsibilities of members of a school community is that they should do what they can to help the victims of bullying. Here are some considerations that may affect **how** and **what** help might be given.

1. If a person has voluntarily come to you for help, it is most likely that you **can** help, if only by listening sympathetically. This is often all that the victim wants. We know that such help can be effective in reducing the negative impact bullying can have on a victim's physical or psychological wellbeing[1].

2. Be aware that on occasions the victim may be unwittingly provoking others and bringing on the bullying. This needs to be tactfully explored. Sometimes what the child needs is to develop skills of fitting in and making good friends.

3. When appropriate, offer practical advice on how the victim can learn to cope more effectively[2]. Remember that if victims can solve the problem unaided the rise in self-esteem is phenomenal. Assertiveness training is useful. But encouraging a victimised child to devise and deliver telling insults (a way of responding recommended by some anti-bullying gurus) can, in many cases, be to a child's disadvantage, especially if the child is being bullied by a stronger, physically aggressive person or by a group. In addition, such responding will certainly contribute to the general level of verbal abuse going on in a school.

4. It may be that the victim needs specialised help; for instance, he or she may be suffering from chronic anxiety, acute depression or from a post-traumatic stress disorder, in which case an appropriate referral should be made[3].

5. Upon close examination, it may be that intervention on the victim's behalf with the bully or bullies is needed. This is likely to be the case if the bullying is particularly severe or hurtful and action on the part of the victim is extremely unlikely to be effective; for instance, if a group of bullies is involved. In such cases, the victim's permission should normally be sought to initiate intervention with the bully or bullies in accordance with agreed school procedures.

6. In extreme cases – for example when very serious and health threatening bullying occurs – it may be decided that action must be taken without the victim's approval.

7. Make sure that records are kept of what has been done to help victimised children, and that the actions and outcomes are communicated, where appropriate, to interested parties, especially parents.

31) HELPING THE BULLIES

Bullies need 'help', not only because their behaviour is damaging to others but also because of the harm that may be done to them as a consequence of them engaging in delinquent behaviour that brings them into conflict with the law[1].

Not all people who bully do so for the same reasons (see Section 13). Hence, individual bullies may be helped in different ways as described below:

1. Some individuals engage in bullying because they want somebody to do something for them and lack the necessary **social skills** to acquire what they want. They do not know how to act in such a way as to elicit positive reactions towards them or to gain another's cooperation. For a minority of students who bully, social skill programs are useful (see Notes, Section 14, note 3).

2. Often students who bully have had little or no experience of enjoying cooperating with others and sharing in the achievement of a common goal[2]. So the provision of opportunities to engage in **cooperative learning** is important for them[3].

3. Students who bully sometimes have a strong need to lead or control others and they may be enabled to occupy roles which give them the opportunity to **exercise power in a socially desirable way**, for example in training or supervising other students in sporting activities. Students who have had a reputation for bullying others have sometimes reformed and taken a leading role in school anti-bullying committees. Care must be taken, however, that such power is not abused but exercised responsibly.

4. Where bullying is largely a result of inadequate **impulse control**, students can sometimes be helped through exercises promoting more thoughtful delayed responses[4]. Socially desirable impulse control can be increased by systematic reinforcement of children's behaviour that is responsible and controlled.

5. Where bullying is a conforming response, seen as enjoyable because one is part of a group, change may sometimes be brought about through sessions with individual bullies who can be brought to act responsibly and discontinue bullying. **The Method of Shared Concern** is one way in which this may be achieved[5].

6. Family life sometimes engenders a tendency to bully others, either because family members model such behaviour or because home life is so frustrating that children wish to take it out on others[6]. Through **interactions with parents**, school staff may have some (albeit limited) influence on how a parent can best bring up their children.

7. Students who bully may change if they identify with powerful and – to them – attractive individuals who consistently act pro-socially. Hence by drawing attention to such **pro-social models** a 'bully' may come to act more like the person he or she admires. Often these are sporting heroes.

32) WORKING CONSTRUCTIVELY WITH PARENTS[1]

School staff and parents may get together on bullying issues as a result of

(i) parents participating in the development of school policy,

(ii) parents expressing concern about their child's involvement in bully/victim problems, usually as a victim, or

(iii) the school requesting a meeting with parents of children who are bullying.

A basic right of parents is to speak with school staff if they believe their child is being bullied at school.

When the parents of victimised children meet with school staff, the following points are relevant

1. Recognise that the parent is generally under a good deal of stress.

2. If a parent expresses anger directed at the school, remain understanding.

3. Make it clear that you do care and will do what you can.

4. Try to get the facts provided by the parent as clear as you can, but don't cross-examine or unduly emphasise inconsistencies in the parent's version of events.

5. Point out that you will need a little time (try to be specific) to investigate the matter yourself, but that you will certainly make contact again soon. There may, however, be some circumstances, when a child's personal safety is severely threatened when action needs to be taken immediately.

6. Assure the parent of the existence of a school policy on bullying – if necessary, explain what it is – and the readiness of the school to take action against bullying.

7. Try to avoid getting into any argument, and above all don't set out to blame the parent, even if you suspect that the parent contributed to the problem.

8. Make it clear that you would be happy to see the parent again, if required.

With the parents of bullies

1. Make sure that you already have as much reliable information about what has happened as you can.

2. Share your concern about what has been happening to the victim.

3. Avoid suggesting that it is the character of their child that is at fault. Rather emphasise that it is aspects of the behaviour of the perpetrator that must change. Try to refer to positive aspects of the child as well.

4. If it is decided that serious consequences for the perpetrator are to follow, for example suspension, point out that if there are no further episodes, the offence will no longer be part of his or her school record.

5. Be understanding, but firm.

> **Note:** Except under special and justified circumstances, it is generally not helpful for the parents of bullies and victims to meet to solve the problem.

TYPES OF SCHOOLS

The suggestions for countering bullying in this handbook apply to all schools in a general way whether they are Primary or Secondary, Coeducational or Single Sex, Private or Public, Boarding or non-Boarding. All kinds of schools should engage in educating their community about bullying, and especially in discovering what is happening among their own members; developing an anti-bullying policy with widespread community support; ensuring that teachers talk with students, encouraging and empowering them to help eliminate bullying; providing support for members who are victimised; intervening, as appropriate, when bullying behaviour is identified; and working sensitively with parents.

However, in applying these practices, it is necessary to recognise differences due to context, as outlined below:

1. Reliable information about bullying from very young children is best obtained through direct observational methods rather than by questionnaires.

2. Generally children at Primary level are more interested in discussing the issue of bullying in class[1]. Different approaches are needed when working with Secondary School classes.

3. In Primary Schools, responsibility for dealing with bully/victim problems is apt to fall more upon a particular teacher who has continual class contact with a group of children and knows each one of them well. Hence, in Secondary Schools there is a stronger need for teachers to share information about students with each other.

4. Large schools can pose a tough challenge in getting everyone behind an agreed school policy to counter bullying. Greater planning may also be needed to implement the policy.

5. Although bullying is reported as happening more often in Primary Schools, students there are more likely to go to staff for help and also receive more effective help in solving their problem[2]. Secondary Schools face a greater challenge in providing appropriate help for victimised students, especially for students in their first two years, when bullying is experienced most often.

6. Bullying tends to be somewhat lower among girls in single sex schools[3]. However, the bullying is often 'relational', subtle, hurtful and psychologically damaging. It more frequently involves bullying conducted by groups. Talking through serious forms of bullying with groups of girls should be a strong priority.

7. Boarding schools provide more opportunities for sustained bullying to occur without respite. If senior students are given responsibilities for supervising the activities of younger children, clear limits must be placed on any disciplinary powers they have, and careful monitoring of abuses in relationships is essential.

8. Although sexual harassment is found among junior students, even in kindergartens, problems of sexual harassment become more common with advancing physiological maturity, and must continually be addressed.

ADVICE FOR PARENTS

When parents discover that their child has been involved in bullying at school, either as a victim or as a bully, it can be very upsetting for them. They may feel at a loss. The school can provide advice to such parents along these lines:

1. If you suspect that your child is being bullied at school, encourage him or her to talk to you about it[1]. Recognise that it may be hard for the child to speak out.

2. Never dismiss the matter by saying that it's the child's problem and he or she must simply stand up to the bully or bullies. Sometimes this course of action is impractical, especially if a group of bullies is involved.

3. Don't be too over-protective either, for example by saying: 'Never mind. I will look after you. You don't have to go to school. Stay home with us.'

4. Listen carefully and sympathetically. Try to get the relevant facts without interrogating the child.

5. Explore alternative courses of action with the child; for example, acting more assertively, making friends who can help, speaking with a teacher or counsellor about it.

6. Decide whether it is best to discuss the problem with the school. This will normally depend upon: (i) the severity of the victimisation, including its duration, (ii) whether it is thought that the child can learn to cope, and (iii) the wishes of the child regarding whether the issue should be raised with the school. On occasions, if the bullying is particularly severe, you may reasonably ask the school for advice despite the reluctance of the child to seek such help.

7. If it is decided that the issue should be raised at school, be prepared to describe as accurately as possible what has been happening to your child.

8. Remember that the school needs to know what has been happening to your child for the good of all other children at the school. Also that the school has a 'duty of care' and is obliged to act 'in loco parentis'[2].

9. You should be assured that the case of bullying you describe will be carefully investigated and dealt with in accordance with the school's Anti-Bullying Policy.

10. If you discover that your child is bullying others at school, take the matter very seriously and exercise whatever influence you can to stop this behaviour.

11. If the school informs you that your child has been bullying others and requests an interview, be prepared to work out a plan with the school to bring about a change in your child's bullying behaviour.

35) A CHECK LIST

This check list enables you to make an assessment of how adequately your school has responded to the issue of bullying. Check how well it has done against each of the items below.

	Inadequately	Adequately	Outstandingly
1. Acquired useful resources for educating the school community about bullying			
2. Taken steps to gather facts about bullying at your school			
3. Developed school policy by involving: Staff Students Parents			
4. Produced an Anti-Bullying Policy which: (i) Describes what bullying is (ii) Recognises the rights of individuals to be safe from being bullied (iii) Stresses the responsibility of everyone to help counter bullying (iv) Indicates how bullying incidents will, in general terms, be dealt with (v) Has the support of the school community			
5. Staff have discussed bullying with students			
6. Victimised students have been supported			
7. Incidents of bullying have been handled			
8. Students have been empowered to take part in action to counter bullying			
9. Students have acted to counter bullying			
10. Constructive meetings have been held with parents on issues of bullying			
11. Overall the school has been responding to bullying			
12. Plans made to review the anti-bullying work			

NOTES

SECTION 1   THE PURPOSE OF THE HANDBOOK

1. An examination of the legal responsibilities of schools in relation to bullying has been provided in an article by Slee & Ford (1999), 'Bullying is a serious issue – It is a crime', in the *Australia and New Zealand Journal of Law and Education*.

SECTION 3   WHY BOTHER ?

1. See Rigby (1996, 1997a) for survey results of bullying in Australian schools. Smith et al. (1999) have provided accounts of surveys conducted throughout the world.

2. Studies of the effects of bullying on children's mental health may be found in Olweus (1993), Rigby & Slee (1993) and Rigby (1998a, 1998b, 1998c, 1999a).

3. Social maladjustment has been found to be a consequence, not simply a cause, of peer victimisation among young children (Kochenderfer & Ladd, 1996).

4. Absenteeism due to bullying at school in Australia is reported by approximately 6% of boys and 9% of girls (Rigby, 1997b).

5. A significant increase in physical health complaints as a consequence of being bullied in the first two years of high school was reported as occurring in an Australian coeducational school (Rigby, 1999a).

6. An enduring loss of self-esteem and proneness to depression was reported among young adults who had been seriously bullied as schoolchildren (Olweus, 1992).

7. The potential for violence by alienated victims, rejected by mainstream peers, was tragically actualised in the shootings at Columbine High School, USA in 1999.

8. Schools vary hugely in the extent to which they experience peer victimisation, with some schools reporting more than three times as much as others (see Rigby, 1996, 1997d).

9. Successful interventions to reduce bullying in schools are described in Olweus (1994), Smith & Sharp (1994) and Petersen & Rigby (1999).

UNDERSTANDING BULLYING

SECTION 4   WHAT IS BULLYING ?

1. One well-known definition of bullying is 'the wilful, conscious desire to hurt another and put him/her under stress' (Tattum & Tattum, 1992). However, this is not adequate as it supposes that such a desire is perfectly correlated with action. In fact, most schoolchildren who admit to wanting to hurt others do not engage in bullying (Rigby, 1997b).

2. The notion that bullying involves a power imbalance has been accepted by most researchers e.g. Olweus (1993) and Farrington (1993).

3. Recognising that bullying is unjust is evident in a useful definition of bullying offered by Smith & Sharp (1994): 'Bullying is the systematic abuse of power'.

4. Whether to recognise as bullying only those actions that are repeated is controversial. Olweus (1993) has argued that we should only include as bullying negative actions that are repeated, and thereby exclude relatively trivial 'one-off' experiences. However, a single occurrence of bullying can sometimes be severe and even traumatising. While bullying typically involves repeated behaviour, common usage allows us to speak of bullying occurring on a single occasion.

5. Enjoyment of the effects of bullying is commonly regarded as characteristic of

bullies. This is true particularly of what has been described as the 'malign' bully with whom we are generally most concerned. But bear in mind that what is seen as bullying behaviour by outsiders is sometimes not intentionally hurtful and not enjoyed. This can be described as non-malign bullying (Rigby, 1996).

6. The notion that 'oppression' is an essential component of bullying was introduced by the British criminologist, Farrington (1993) who defined bullying as 'repeated oppression, psychological or physical, of a less powerful person by a more powerful person'. He neglected to add 'or group of persons'.

SECTION 5   GENDER, RACE, DISABILITY AND SOCIAL CLASS

1. As an example, see the anti-discrimination and anti-harassment policy document provided for schools by the Education Department of Tasmania (April 2000). See Gilbert & Gilbert (1998) for a good discussion of the construction of masculinty among schoolchildren and how it can lead to bullying.

3. A comprehensive report on sex-based harassment in Australia is included in *Gender and School Education* by Collins, Batten, Ainley, & Getty (1996).

4. An analysis of data from a recent study by Rigby & Bagshaw of Year 9 students (190 boys and 217 girls) attending coeducational schools in South Australia indicates that 53.1% of girls reported having been verbally abused or 'called names' by boys during the school year compared with 25.9% of boys who report similar treatment from girls. Thus verbal abuse runs both ways, but is predominantly from boys to girls.

5. Fazal Rizvi (1998) has provided a useful analysis of racism in Australia, especially in relation to Aboriginal and Torres Strait Island Australians and Asian Australians.

6. Some studies have reported a greater incidence of verbal abuse directed towards students of non-mainstream ethnic background. For example, Boulton (1995) in one study found that Asian students in England were subjected to more racial name-calling than were other students. However, another study, conducted in Germany by Losel & Bliesener (1999), reported that students of non-German extraction were treated by their peers the same as others. Furthermore, survey results from Australia using the PRQ (Rigby, unpublished) with children aged 8 to 11 years did not reveal differences in reported peer victimisation between children identified as from non-English speaking backgrounds and others. The results for Aboriginal boys in this latter study nevertheless did indicate for them a significantly high level of peer victimisation compared with other boys. Clearly, the country and the specific ethnic groups involved may make a crucial difference.

7. Mooney & Smith (1995) reported that the bullying of children who stammer sometimes affected them for many years, even into adult years.

8. As in studies of ethnic differences and bullying, studies of the relationship between social class and bullying are inconsistent. For example, in the United Kingdom Whitney & Smith (1993) and Mellor (1999) have provided evidence that children in schools in low socioeconomic areas are more likely than others to be victimised; studies from Norway (Olweus, 1999) and Spain (Ortega & Mora-Mechan, 1999) suggest that socioeconomic status is unrelated to bullying. It has been suggested, however, that the nature of the bullying may differ according to social class, with children from lower socioeconomic class families being more prone to bully others physically, but currently evidence is lacking on this point.

SECTION 6   POWER INEQUALITIES

1. The importance of sheer physical size and strength as a factor in bullying behaviour has been researched by Olweus (1993).

2. Relational aggression is a term coined by American psychologists Crick & Grotpeter (1995) to describe acts of aggression designed to manipulate and damage another's relationship with peers, and is believed to be practised more by girls.

SECTION 7   WHEN FORCEFULNESS IS NOT BULLYING

1. What is seen as acceptable treatment in one generation may be unacceptable in the next. For thousands of years slavery, now seen as a systematic and unacceptable abuse of power, was practised in many societies. In the 19th Century the use of 'fags' by senior schoolboys was practised in British Public Schools (see Rigby, 1997c), and remnants of this system are still to be found in some schools where senior students are given, and sometimes abuse, privileges.

SECTION 9   SEXUAL HARASSMENT

1. For detailed examination of sexual harassment in schools see the New South Wales Department of School Education (1996). Herbert (1992) discusses ways of countering such harassment in schools.

2. Although cross-gender harassment is experienced somewhat more often by girls, boys are not uncommonly harassed sexually by other boys. Both sexes appear equally upset by it. In an unpublished study of 613 Year 9 Secondary School students in South Australia (Rigby & Bagshaw, 1999) some 33% of girls and 19% of boys reported that they had been the target of unwanted sexual remarks during the school year. Of these, approximately 85% of each sex said they had been upset by it. Some 20% of girls and 18% of boys claimed to have been sexually harassed by the opposite sex. Boy–boy harassment was reported by 13% of boys; girl–girl by only 2% of girls. Unwanted sexual touching was reported by 12% of boys and 12% of girls.

SECTION 10   BULLYING AS A DYNAMIC PROCESS

1. For a discussion of the characteristics of victims see Rigby (1996, pp. 72–3).

SECTION 11   THE PASSIVE VICTIM

1. Typically when bullying occurs there is an audience of bystanders. According to feedback from Australian students, most bystanders encourage the bullies either actively (verbally encouraging) or passively by being interested watchers. Relatively few support the victim. Similar results were found using direct behavioural observations in Canada by O'Connell, Pepler & Craig (1999).

2. Surveys of senior students (16–18 years) in Australia indicate that some 8% of boys and 6% of girls were bullied continually by another person or group for a year or more (Rigby, 1997b).

SECTION 12   THE RESISTANT VICTIM

1. According to a large-scale Australian survey, approximately 10% of students across all age groups claimed that 'telling' someone made matters worse. The success rate for 'telling', however, is much greater for younger Primary School students. Only a minority of Secondary students appear to be helped by telling:

typically for older students it makes no difference to what happens (Rigby, 1997b).

2. It has been claimed that some well known entertainers, such as Robin Williams, Dudley Moore and Clive James, developed their talent to amuse and distract as a defence against bullies. But how many must have failed to do so!

SECTION 13   WHY SOME PEOPLE BULLY

1. Bullies typically believe that they are admired for what they do, often on good evidence (Rigby, 1997d).

2. According to the behaviourist Skinner (1953), the submission of others is highly reinforcing for humans as well as for animals.

3. It is sometimes pointed out that in our society boys typically construct and conform to a 'macho' image of masculinity which leads them to engage in acts of aggression and bullying (see Gilbert & Gilbert, 1998). Unfortunately, increasing numbers of girls also construct an image of toughness that can have the same effect.

4. Approximately 30% of boys and 20% of girls in High Schools report that for them bullying others would be fun (Rigby, 1997b).

5. Bullies tend to score higher than average on Eysenck's measure of Psychoticism, which reflects a low level of concern for the pain experienced by others (Slee & Rigby, 1993). They also score low on measures of Empathy (Farley, 1999).

6. Reliable links have been found repeatedly between bullying others at school and unsatisfactory home life where students have felt badly treated (see Olweus, 1980; Rigby, 1994).

7. Many studies have linked viewing violence on television with subsequent aggression. For instance, an American study (Singer et al., 1999) of elementary and middle school students found that children who were frequently exposed to violence on television were more likely to engage in violent behaviour. This was so especially when there was a lack of parental monitoring.

8. When asked why they might bully someone, a majority of children say that they do so 'to get even' (Rigby, 1997b).

9. Researchers in the area of stress claim that some people are 'aggressively involved in a chronic, incessant struggle to achieve more and more in less and less time, and, if required to do so, against the opposing efforts of other things and persons' (Friedman & Rosenman, 1974). Such so-called Type A personalities are prone to engage in bullying behaviours to get things done at all costs.

10. Much bullying is carried out by people who are obediently following orders, even when the orders appear inhumane and unjustified. See Milgram (1974) for the classic study of obedience to authority.

11. People may define their role so as to include bullying behaviour. See the famous experiment by Zimbardo (1972) in which American college students simulated the roles of prison officers and behaved automatically as sadistic bullies. We need continually to clarify and reflect on our role behaviours.

SECTION 14   WHY SOME PEOPLE DO NOT BULLY

1. Some 80% of boys and 70% of girls in Australian schools believe that they are in fact no less able than other students to bully (Rigby, 1997b). We know from various studies that most students do not engage in bullying others. This clearly

suggests that a large proportion of those who can bully, simply do not do so.

2. Approximately 50% of Australian Secondary School children indicated that they would feel ashamed of themselves if they bullied someone (Rigby, 1997d).

3. Social skills programs can be helpful in cases where conflict arises because of a lack of knowledge of alternative, more appropriate ways of behaving. See Macmullin (1999) for an account of how a social skills program can be developed for use in schools. But bear in mind that well-honed social skills can sometimes be employed effectively in bullying others, especially in relational bullying.

ACTION TO COUNTER BULLYING

SECTION 15 SETTING GOALS

1. As an example of how the effects of bullying can be assessed in a school, see Petersen & Rigby (1999).

SECTION 17 EDUCATING THE SCHOOL COMMUNITY

1. Here is a short list of books, articles and videos that are particularly useful in providing a background to the study of bullying in schools:

Olweus, D. (1993). *Bullying at school.* Cambridge: Blackwell.

Rigby, K. (1996). *Bullying in schools – and what to do about it.* Camberwell, Melbourne: Australian Council for Educational Research.

Rigby, K. (1999b). *Bullying in schools: Guidelines to effective action.* Professional reading guide for educational administrators, 21(1, Feb/March).

Sharp, S., & Smith, P.K. (Eds.). (1994) *Tackling bullying in your school: A practical handbook for teachers.* London: Routledge.

Smith, P.K et al. (Eds.). (1999). *The nature of school bullying: A cross-national perspective.* London: Routledge.

Queensland Department of Education. (1998). *Bullying – no way! A professional developmental resource for school communities.* Brisbane: Queensland Department of Education.

Queensland Department of Education. (1998). *Bullying – no way! A professional developmental resource for school communities* [Video].

An Internet site which enables users to access information for school educators from a wide range of sources throughout the world can be found at http://www.education.unisa.edu.au/bullying/educators.html

2. The Queensland Education Department video (see reference above) is an excellent resource for focusing discussion on ways in which students bully in schools. It consists of 21 vignettes enacting bullying incidents that occur in Primary and Secondary Schools. Viewers are invited to comment on each of them, and discussion may follow using questions provided in an accompanying book of the same title. The videos are intended as part of a professional development process for school personnel. This invaluable resource is available from Open Access Unit, Education Services Directorate, Education Queensland. P.O. Box 220, Ashgrove, Queensland, 4006. Tel: (07) 3377 1000; Fax: (07) 3366 3849.

3. Recently a number of schools have trained students to become peer mediators and/or peer counsellors to help students involved in bully/victim problems. How this can be done is demonstrated in two excellent videos, one made by the Education Dept of New South Wales (1998) which shows how students can help

to resolve conflicts between peers, and the other by Jane Balfour (1994), which shows how peer counselling on bullying issues can be handled by students.

4. Ideas for lesson planning with Primary School children relevant to bullying can be found in Murphy, E., & Lewers, R. (2000), and Garrity, Jens, Porter, Sager, & Short-Camilli (1997). For older students, see Jenkin (1996) and New South Wales Department of School Education (1996).

5. Videos on bullying that can engage the attention of Primary School students include two videos available through Video Education Australia: *Keith: A story of a Bully* (1995) and No more teasing (1999), a helpful account of how children can respond effectively to low level bullying. An intriguing video called *Only Playing, Miss!* by the Neti-Neti Theatre Company (1990) is excellent for engaging the interest of older students and promoting discussion. Finally, for students who are soon to leave school or are undertaking 'work experience,' there is a good video, *No bull* featuring students reflecting on the bullying that they had encountered during their short experience in the workplace, produced by the Victorian Employers Chamber of Commerce and Job Watch Inc. (1999).

6. Information on the Internet, provided mainly by people who have been bullied at school – often students – can be found at http://www.education.unisa.edu.au/bullying/students.html

7. Some useful advice for students who are being bullied at school can be found in books by Stones (1993), Elliott (1998) and Field (1999).

8. There are some 90 000 Safety Houses in Australia.
See http://www.nhwatch.asn.au/child1.htm#bully for useful Internet information. Contact the Safety House Association in your State for detailed information.

9. Books which contain advice for parents include Byrne (1996) and Rigby (1996).

10. Helpful resources can be accessed through the Internet.
See http://www.education.unisa.edu.au/bullying/parents.html

11. The Australian Council for Educational Research Limited (ACER) hold a range of books and videos on bullying and can be consulted on the availability of resources on bullying, including the provision of workshops and seminars. Their contact is: Private Bag 55, Camberwell, Victoria, Australia. Tel: (03) 9835 7447; Fax: (03) 9835 7499; email: sales@acer.edu.au.

SECTION 19   HOW TO GET THE FACTS

1. It is important to make use of reliable, valid and anonymously administered questionnaires. Otherwise the information may be of dubious value and misleading. Also, with non-anonymous questionnaires, as in so-called Bully Audits, there is a real danger that a child may be inappropriately and unfairly labelled as a bully with serious consequences for that child's future.

SECTION 20   DEVELOPING AN ANTI-BULLYING POLICY

1. Examples of school policies in Australia can be found in Rigby (1996, pp. 136–40) and see Tattum & Herbert (1993) for examples of school policies in England.

SECTION 22   WHAT TEACHERS CAN DO ABOUT BULLYING

1. Good classroom management skills are essential in countering the tendency of some students to bully others. Where there is disrespectful and disorderly behaviour in a classroom there is abundant opportunity for some students to engage

in bullying without necessarily being detected by the teacher. While many teachers learn 'on the job' and become more efficient with practice, some teachers need help, for some time, from more experienced teachers who can act as observers. Some excellent texts on classroom management are available, for example Rogers (1997) and Latham (1997).

2. The leading authors on cooperative learning are the brothers, David and Roger Johnson. Their work has been applied in many schools and validated by high quality research. Good practical advice on cooperative learning is available in Johnson & Johnson (1992).

SECTION 23 TALKING WITH STUDENTS IN CLASS ABOUT BULLYING

1. See note 1 Section 33 on school differences.

2. The use of role-play can be a particularly powerful way of raising awareness of bullying and examining ways in which students can respond more effectively when someone tries to bully them or when, as bystanders, they may want to help someone who is being bullied. *The Hidden Hurt* by Murphy & Lewers (2000) provides suggestions for relevant role-plays as well as class exercises designed to help children, especially of Primary School age.

SECTION 24 ROLES FOR EMPOWERED STUDENTS

1. The concept of an Anti-Bullying Committee of students led by a staff member has been developed and employed effectively at Jamisson High School in New South Wales, Australia by Ms L. Petersen. Tel: (02) 4731 6144. For a description of this work, see Petersen & Rigby (1999).

SECTION 25 WHAT STUDENTS CAN DO

1. Whether suitably trained students should perform the role of mediator in resolving bully/victim problems is a controversial issue. Interested educators should certainly view the video *Bullying* by Jane Balfour (1994) – obtainable from ACER – which describes in detail how senior students at an English school successfully undertook this task. Also read *Peer counselling in schools* by Cowie & Sharp (1996).

SECTION 26 ACCESSING USEFUL RESOURCES

1. Information about Peer Support can be obtained from http://www.peersupport.edu.au and http://www.peersupport.com.au/peace_schools.htm

2. There are two outstanding publications on conflict resolution in schools by Johnson & Johnson (1991) and Bodine, Crawford & Schrumpf (1994).

3. See Bagshaw & Halliday (2000) on teaching adolescents to handle conflict through drama.

4. A full description of where training in dispute resolution can be obtained can be accessed through http://www.ausdispute.unisa.edu.au/education.htm

5. The New South Wales Department of School Education has produced an excellent introductory video: *Peer mediation for primary school children. We can work it out.* The Department also provides training in peer mediation for interested schools. In South Australia, Ms Pam Harrison provides a similar service: contact marionls@senet.com.au

SECTION 27 BULLY/VICTIM CASES

1. Whether more bullying is done by individuals acting alone or by groups is controversial. From survey data from 38 000 Australian schoolchildren, aged 7 to 17 years (Rigby, 1997b), it was found that victims tended to report being bullied more often by individuals, while bullies claimed that they more often bullied others when they were part of a group.

2. For a case study of the serial bully, see Tony Parker's (1990) vivid account of Big Bully Billy (*Life after life*), an aggressive bully who, as an adult, was imprisoned for murder.

3. For accounts of teachers as bullies, see autobiographical accounts of their schooldays by C.S. Lewis (1975) and Roald Dahl (1991).

4. For a dramatisation of bullying by a leader and accomplice, see the video *Only Playing, Miss!* (1990) (see page 51). Such bullying can sometimes have tragic consequences, as in the case of the duo of children, Robert Thompson and Jon Venables, who bullied and murdered the two-year-old James Bulger in England in 1993.

5. This is a quite common scenario. See Pikas (1999) for a description of the dynamics of such groups.

6. According to British researcher Andrew Terry (1998), over 50% of teachers report that they have been bullied by a pupil or pupils at least once, with 10% reporting that it happens to them several times a week.

7. Fraser Harrison's (1989) autobiography includes a moving account of the inane and thoughtless bullying of an 'outsider' at an English boarding school.

8. One group bullying another group is the theme of *Revenge of the nerds* (1984), a cult movie directed by Jeff Kanew. This is a light-hearted but oddly perceptive film about the 'war' between American Geeks and their tormentors, the Jocks.

SECTION 29 ALTERNATIVE TREATMENTS

1. The so-called No Blame Approach was devised by Maines & Robinson (1992) and is described in their video. An extension of this approach called the Support Group Approach was developed more recently by Sue Young. Descriptions of each can be accessed through http://www.education.unisa.edu.au/bullying/

2. The Method of Shared Concern was developed by Professor Anatol Pikas at Uppsala University, Sweden. For descriptions see Rigby (1996) and the above website. Successful applications of this method have been conducted at Jamisson High School in NSW by Ms L Petersen.

3. An application of a 'consequences-based' approach in elementary schools is described by Garrity, Jens, Porter, Sager, & Short-Camilli (1994).

4. Community Conferencing is a method originally developed in New Zealand for resolving relatively serious offences through a conference to which victims, offenders, and family were invited in lieu of a court procedure. A description of how it operates, supplied by an experienced practitioner of the method, Dr David Moore, can be accessed through my website. In New South Wales, School Community Forums have been introduced as a possible alternative to suspension.

SECTION 30 HELPING THE VICTIMS

1. The buffering effect of social support in diminishing the damage that bullying can produce on the mental health of children has been examined in Rigby & Slee (1999) and Rigby (2000).

2. Some practical advice for children who can learn to be assertive may be found in Field (1999), Berne (1996) and Stones (1993). One needs to be careful, however, to make suggestions appropriate to the child and the situation the child is in.

3. Some specialised help can be obtained through Kids Help Line, which is staffed with experienced counsellors who frequently deal with problems of bullying among children. Toll Free Number: 1 800 5518000. All children should know about this service.

SECTION 31 HELPING THE BULLIES

1. From Scandinavian research (Olweus, 1993) we learn that children identified as bullies at school are up to four times more likely than others to come before the courts subsequently on charges of delinquency.

2. We know from the research of Rigby, Cox & Black (1997) that many children who bully have had few, if any, positive experiences of working cooperatively with others and need to be carefully persuaded to do so in rewarding circumstances.

3. An account of how cooperative learning was introduced in schools in England in an attempt to reduce bullying is given in a book by Cowie, Smith, Boulton & Laver (1994).

4. See in particular the 'Stop, Think, Do' program pioneered successfully by Linda Petersen (1994) in Australia.

5. The Method of Shared Concern of Anatol Pikas is described fully in the website http://www.education.unisa.edu.au/bullying.

6. The relationship between dysfunctional family life and the engagement of Australian adolescents bullying in schools is examined in Rigby (1993).

SECTION 32 WORKING CONSTRUCTIVELY WITH PARENTS

1. A further discussion of working with parents is in Rigby (1996), pp. 240–50.

SECTION 33 TYPES OF SCHOOLS

1. In Primary Schools approximately 50% of students are positively in favour of class discussions about bullying. In Secondary Schools the percentage drops to about 27% in Year 9, but rises to 35% in Year 11. Note that many children are 'on the fence'. Notably for every Year group, girls are more interested in such discussions (Rigby, 1997b).

2. Children who are bullied in Primary School are much more likely to report that the help they receive is more effective in solving their problem (Rigby, 1997b).

3 See Rigby (1998d) for a discussion of gender and bullying in schools.

SECTION 34 ADVICE FOR PARENTS

1. A list of warning signs that a child is being bullied at school is given in Rigby (1996) p. 240.

2. 'In loco parentis' means that the school is acting (or should be acting) in place of you 'as a parent' and has a duty to take reasonable care of your child. For the legal implications see Slee & Ford (1999).

REFERENCES

Bagshaw, D., & Halliday, D. (in press). Teaching adolescents to handle conflict through drama. *Asian Pacific Teacher Education Journal.*

Berne, S. (1996). *Bully-proof your child.* Melbourne: Lothian.

Bodine, R.J., Crawford, D.K., & Schrumpf, F. (1994). *Creating the peaceable school: A comprehensive program for teaching conflict resolution.* Champain, Illinois: Research Press.

Boulton, M.J. (1995). Patterns of bully/victim problems in mixed race groups of children. *Social Development, 4,* 277–93.

Collins, C., Batten, M., Ainley, J., & Getty, C. (1996). *Gender and school education.* Melbourne: Australian Council for Educational Research Ltd (ACER).

Cowie, H., & Sharp, S. (1996). *Peer conselling in schools. London:* David Fulton.

Cowie, H., Smith, P.K., Boulton, M., & Laver, R. (1994). *Cooperation in the multi-ethnic classroom.* London: David Fulton.

Crick, N.R., & Grotpeter, J K. (1995). Relational aggression, gender, and social-psychological adjustment. *Child Development, 66*(3) 710–22.

Dahl, R. (1991). *Boy.* New York: Penguin.

Department of Education, Tasmania. (2000). *Anti-discrimination and anti-harassment policy support materials.* Department of Education: Tasmania.

Education Department of New South Wales. (1996). *Resources for teaching against violence* (Revised) (pp. 138–71). Sydney, Australia: New South Wales Department of School Education.

Elliott, M. (1998). *Bullying.* London: Hodder Children's Books.

Farley, R.L. (1999). *Does a relationship exist between social perception, social intelligence and empathy for students with a tendency to be a bully, victim or bully/victim?* Unpublished Honours thesis, Psychology Department, The University of Adelaide.

Farrington, D.P. (1993). Understanding and preventing bullying. In M.Tonny & N. Morris (Eds.), *Crime and justice (Vol 17).* Chicago: University of Chicago Press.

Field, E.M. (1999). *Bully busting.* Lane Cove, Sydney: Finch.

Friedman, M. & Rosenman, R.H. (1974). *Type A behaviour and your heart.* New York: Knopf.

Garrity, C., Jens K., Porter W., Sager, N., & Short-Camilli, C. (1994). *Bully proofing your schools.* Opris West: Longmont, Colorado.

Gilbert, R. & Gilbert, P. (1998). *Masculinity goes to school.*St Leonards, NSW: Allen & Unwin.

Harrison, F. (1989). *Trivial disputes.* London: Collins.

Herbert, Carrie (1992). *Sexual harassment in schools: A guide for teachers.* London: David Fulton.

Jenkin, J. (1996). *Resolving violence: An anti-bullying curriculum for senior students.* Melbourne: Australian Council for Educational Research Ltd.

Johnson, D.W., & Johnson, R.T. (1991). *Teaching students to be peacemakers.* Edina, Minnesota: Interaction Book Company.

Johnson, D.W., & Johnson, R.T. (1992). *Creative controversy: Intellectual challenge in the classroom.* Edina, Minnesota: Interaction Book Company.

Kochenderfer, B.J., & Ladd, G.W. (1996). Peer victimisation: Cause or consequence of school maladjustment. *Child Development, 67,* 1305–13.

Latham, G.I. (1997). *Behind the schoolhouse door: Eight skills every teacher should have*. Logan, Utah: Mountain Plain Regional Resource Center, Utah State University.

Lewis, C.S. (1975). *Surprised by joy: The shape of my early life*. London: Harcourt Brace.

Losel, F., & Bliesener, T. (1999). Germany. In P.K. Smith et al. (Eds.), *The Nature of School Bullying* (pp. 224–49). London: Routledge.

Macmullin, C. (1999). Developing a social skills programme for use in school. In P.T. Sleee & K Rigby (Eds.), *Children's peer relations* (pp. 242–353). London: Routledge.

Mellor, A. (1999). Scotland. In P.K. Smith et al. (Eds.), *The nature of school bullying* (91–111). London: Routledge.

Milgram, S. (1974). *Obedience to authority*. New York: Harper and Rowe.

Mooney, S., & Smith, P.K. (1995). Bullying and the child who stammers. *British Journal of Special Education, 22*, 24–7.

Murphy, E., & Lewers, R. (Eds.) (2000). *The hidden hurt*. Ballarat: Wizard Publication.

O'Connell, P., Pepler, D., & Craig, W. (1999). Peer involvement in bullying: Insights and challenges for intervention. *Journal of Adolescence, 22*, 437–52.

Olweus, D (1980). Familial and temperamental determinants of aggressive behaviour in adolescent boys: A causal analysis. *Developmental Psychology, 16*, 644–60.

Olweus, D. (1992). Victimisation by peers: Antecedents and long term outcomes. In K.H. Rubin & J.B. Asendorf (Eds.). *Social withdrawal, inhibition and shyness in children* (pp. 315–42). Hillsdale, N.J.:Erlbaum.

Olweus, D. (1993). *Bullying at school: What we know and what we can do*. Cambridge, MA: Blackwell.

Olweus, D. (1994). Bullying at school: Basic facts and effects of a school based intervention program. *Journal of Child Psychology and Psychiatry, 35*, 1171–90.

Olweus, D. (1999). Norway. In P.K. Smith et al. (Eds.), *The nature of school bullying* (28–48). London: Routledge.

Ortega, R., & Mora-Mechan, J.A. (1999). Spain. In P.K. Smith et al. (Eds.), *The nature of school bullying* (pp. 157–73). London: Routledge.

Parker, T. (1990). *Life after Life*. London: Harper Collins.

Peterson, L. (Linda) (1994). Stop and think learning: Motivating learning in social groups and individuals. In Mark Tainsh & John Izard (Eds.), *Widening Horizons: New Challenges, Directions and Achievements* (pp. 70–83). Melbourne: The Australian Council for Educational Research Limited.

Petersen, L (Libby), & Rigby, K. (1999). Countering bullying at an Australian secondary school. *Journal of Adolescence, 22*(4), 481–92.

Pikas, A. (1999). New developments of shared concern method. *School Psychology International*, 1–19.

Queensland Department of Education. (1998). *Bullying – no way! A professional developmental resource for school communities*. Brisbane: Queensland Department of Education.

Rigby, K. (1993). School children's perceptions of their families and parents as a function of peer relations. *Journal of Genetic Psychology, 154*(4), 501–14.

Rigby, K (1994). Psycho-social functioning in families of Australian adolescent schoolchildren involved in bully/victim problems, *Journal of Family Therapy, 16*(2) 173–89.

Rigby, K. (1996). *Bullying in schools – and what to do about it*. Melbourne: ACER. (British Edition, 1997, London: Jessica Kingsley).

Rigby, K. (1997a). What children tell us about bullying in schools. *Children Australia, 22*(2), 28–34.

Rigby, K. (1997b). *Manual for the peer relations questionnaire* (PRQ). Point Lonsdale, Victoria, Australia: The Professional Reading Guide.

Rigby, K. (1997c). Reflections on Tom Brown's Schooldays and the problem of bullying today. *Australian Journal of Social Science 4*(1), 85–96.

Rigby, K. (1997d). Attitudes and beliefs about bullying among Australian school children. *Irish Journal of Psychology, 18*(2), 202–20.

Rigby, K. (1998a). The relationship between reported health and involvement in bully/victim problems among male and female secondary school students. *Journal of Health Psychology, 3*(4), 465–76.

Rigby, K. (1998b). Peer relations at school and the health of children. *Youth Studies Australia, 17*(1), 13–17.

Rigby, K. (1998c). Suicidal ideation and bullying among Australian secondary school children. *Australian Educational and Developmental Psychologist, 15*(1), 45–61.

Rigby, K. (1998d). Gender and bullying in schools. In P.T. Slee & K. Rigby (Eds.), *Children's peer relations* (pp. 47–59). London: Routledge.

Rigby, K. (1999a). Peer victimisation at school and the health of secondary students. *British Journal of Educational Psychology, 22*(2), 28–34.

Rigby, K. (1999b). Bullying in schools: Guidelines to effective action. *Professional reading guide for educational administrators, 21*(1, Feb/March).

Rigby, K. (2000). Effects of peer victimisation in schools and perceived social support on adolescent well-being. *Journal of Adolescence, 23*(1), 57–68.

Rigby, K., Cox, I. K., & Black, G. (1997). Cooperativeness and bully/victim problems among Australian schoolchildren. *Journal of Social Psychology*, 137,(3), 357–68.

Rigby, K., & Slee, P.T. (1993). Dimensions of interpersonal relating among Australian school children and their implications for psychological well-being. *Journal of Social Psychology, 133*(1), 33–42.

Rigby, K., & Slee, P.T. (1999). Suicidal ideation among adolescent school children, involvement in bully/victim problems and perceived low social support. *Suicide and Life-threatening Behaviour*, 29, 119–30.

Rizvi, F. (1998). Thinking about racism. In Department of Education, Queensland, *Bullying – no way!* (pp. 42–52). Brisbane: Queensland Department of Education.

Rogers, B. (1997). *'You know the fair rule' and much more* (2nd ed.). Melbourne: ACER.

Smith, P.K., & Sharp, S. (Eds.). (1994). *School bullying: Insights and perspectives*, London: Routledge.

Singer, M.I., Miller, D.B., Guo, S., Flannery, D.J., Frierson, T., & Slovak, K. (1999). Contributors to violent behavior among elementary and middle School. *Pediatrics, 104*(4), 878.

Skinner, B.F. (1953). *Science and human behaviour*. New York: Macmillan.

Slee, P.T., & Ford, D.C. (1999). Bullying is a serious issue – It is a crime. Australia and *New Zealand Journal of Law and Education 4*(1), 23–39.

Slee, P.T., & Rigby, K. (1993). The relationship of Eysenck's personality factors and self-esteem to bully/victim behaviour in Australian schoolboys. *Personality and Individual Differences*, 14, 371–73.

Smith, P.K., & Sharp, S. (Eds.). (1994). *School bullying: Insights and perspectives.* London: Routledge.

Smith, P.K., Morita, J., Junger-Tas, Olweus, D., Catalona, R., & Slee, P.T. (Eds.). (1999). *The nature of school bullying.* London: Routledge.

Stones, R. (1993). *Don't pick on me.* Markham, ON: Pembroke.

Tattum, D., & Herbert, G. (1993). *Countering bullying: Initiatives by schools and local authorities.* Stoke-on-Trent: Trentham.

Tattum, D., & Tattum, E. (1992). *Social education and personal development.* London: David Fulton.

Terry, A.A. (1998). Teachers as targets of bullying by their pupils: A study to investigate incidence. *British Journal of Educational Psychology.* 68, 255–68.

Whitney, I., & Smith, P.K. (1993). A survey of the nature and extent of bullying in junior/middle and secondary schools. *Educational Research, 35,* 3–25

Zimbardo, P.G. (1972). Pathology of imprisonment. *Society,* 4–8.

VIDEOS

Balfour, J. (1994). *Bullying.* Melbourne: Australian Council for Educational Research Limited.

CTE (UK). (1995). *Keith: A story of a bully.* Bendigo, Victoria: Video Education Australia.

Education Department of New South Wales. (1998). *Peer mediation for primary school children. We can work it out.* Sydney: New South Wales Department of Education and Training.

Maines, B., & Robinson, G. (1992). *The no blame approach.* Bristol: Lame Duck Publishing.

Neti-Neti Theatre Company. (1990). *Only playing, miss!* Melbourne: Australian Council for Educational Research Limited.

Queensland Department of Education. (1998). *Bullying – no way! A professional developmental resource for school communities.* (Available from Open Access Unit, Education Services Directorate, Education Queensland. P.O. Box 220, Ashgrove, Queensland, 4006)

Sunburst Communications, USA. (1994). *No more teasing.* Bendigo, Victoria: Video Education Australia.

Victorian Employers Chamber of Commerce and Job Watch Inc. (1999). *No bull.* Hawthorn: Victoria: Open Channel Productions.

Appendix: Sheets for copying

DEFINING BULLYING

BULLYING INVOLVES:

a desire to hurt

+

hurtful action

+

a power imbalance

+

(typically) repetition

+

an unjust use of power

+

evident enjoyment by the aggressor

+

a sense of being oppressed on the part of the victim

THE MEANS OF BULLYING (EXAMPLES)

	DIRECT	INDIRECT
VERBAL ABUSE	Verbal insults	Persuading another person to criticise or insult someone
	Unfair criticism	Spreading malicious rumours
	Name calling	Anonymous phone calls, emails
GESTURAL ABUSE	Threatening or obscene gestures	Deliberate turning away or averting one's gaze to ignore someone
	Menacing stares	
PHYSICAL MEANS	Striking	Getting another person to assault someone
	Throwing things	Removing and hiding belongings
	Using a weapon	
RELATIONAL BULLYING	Overtly forming coalitions against someone	Persuading people to exclude someone

THE BULLY/VICTIM CYCLE

BULLYING AND THE PASSIVE VICTIM

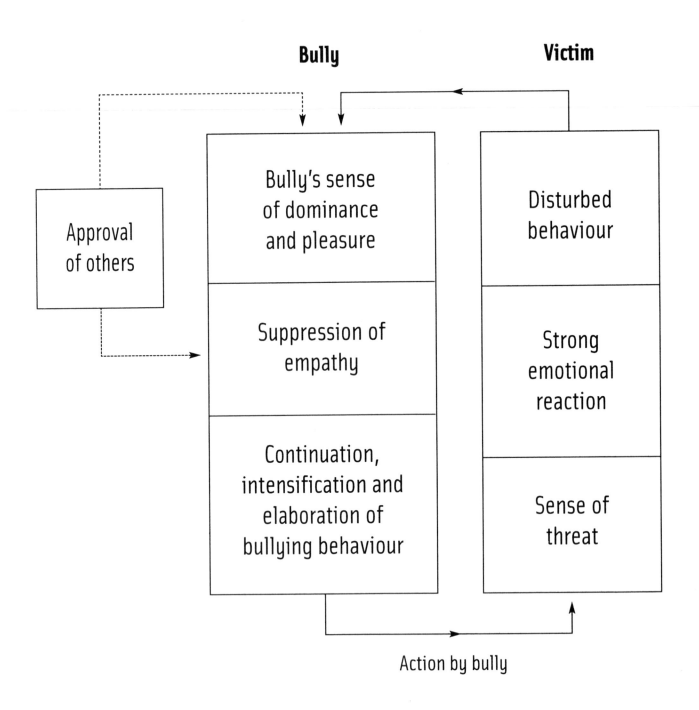

THE BULLY/VICTIM CYCLE (continued)

BULLYING AND THE RESISTANT VICTIM

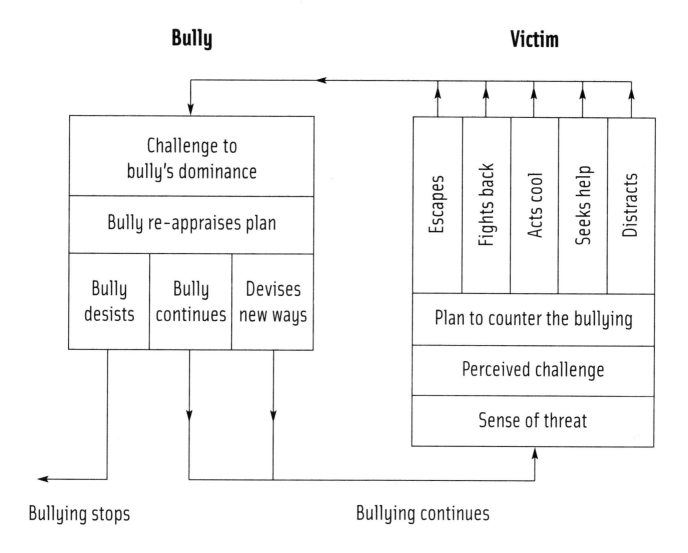

This diagram shows what victims often do to resist being bullied –
sometimes successfully, often not successfully.

WHAT GOES INTO THE POLICY

1. A strong statement of the **school's stand** against bullying.

2. A succinct **definition** of bullying, with illustrations.

3. A declaration of the **rights** of individuals in the school community – students, teachers, other workers and parents – **to be free of bullying** and (if bullied) **to be provided with help and support**.

4. A statement of the **responsibilities** of members of the school community: to **abstain personally from bullying** others in any way, and to **actively discourage bullying** when it occurs.

5. A **general** description of what the school will do **to deal with incidents of bullying**. For example, the severity and seriousness of the bullying will be assessed and appropriate action taken. This may include the use of counselling practices, the imposition of sanctions, interviews with parents and, in extreme cases, suspension from school.

6. An undertaking to **evaluate** the policy in the near and specified future.

ALTERNATIVE APPROACHES TO DEALING WITH BULLIES

1. **Providing and implementing clearly defined rules to apply appropriate 'consequences' (or punishment) for those identified as having bullied someone.** These may range from loss of 'privileges' or imposition of 'chores', to detentions and suspension or exclusion from school.

2. **Counselling.** This may include **informal talks** with the bully seeking to change his or her behaviour. Or it could involve a **more structured approach** of which two have been suggested:

    a) **The No Blame Approach.** This requires groups of children containing the supposed bullies to be convened. Normally there would be a number of influential pro-social children involved. The plight of the victim is described and the group left to come up with a responsible solution. The outcome is then carefully monitored.

    b) **The Method of Shared Concern.** This requires the counsellor to share his or her concern for the 'victim' with individual members of the group and to elicit a promise to act in a specified and positive way in future interactions with the victim. This is done in a non-threatening manner along lines suggested by Professor Anatol Pikas.

3. **School conferencing.** Bullies and victims are brought together at a meeting which their parents and friends also attend. Victims are strongly supported in expressing their objection to how they have been treated. The bully is induced to feel **a sense of shame** and is expected to make appropriate reparations before a reconciliation can be effected.

Note that what you do should depend upon
a) **the sort of bully/victim problem** you have – e.g. its seriousness,
b) t**he school philosophy** on how change can best be produced, and
c) a thorough understanding of **how each method works**.

TWENTY QUESTIONS TO ASK YOURSELF

Here are some questions you may like to address in discussions and in the course of providing a summary of how you think the problem of bullying should be addressed.

1. What consequences of bullying concern you most?
2. How satisfactory is the proposed definition of bullying?
    Can you improve on it?
3. What power inequalities does one have to accept in a school? What power differences at your school might be reduced and thereby minimise bullying?
4. What, if any, expressions of 'forcefulness' in a school should be accepted or at least tolerated?
5. What means of bullying in your school would you most like to stop being exercised? How would you prioritise them?
6. At your school what seem to be the main reasons why children bully?
7. What specific goals would you like to set for your school regarding bullying?
8. What components of the plan suggested in Section 16 would you mark as important for your school? Are there others you would add?
9. What steps do you think your school should take to get the facts about bullying at your school?
10. Is a school policy against bullying justified? If so, what should go into it? Who (staff, parents, students) should be included in helping to develop it?
11. How can teachers be guided and helped to raise the issue of bullying with their classes most effectively?
12. How can curriculum and lesson content help to raise awareness about bullying and help develop skills to counter it?
13. How can students become involved in initiating and taking positive action against bullying? Is forming a School Anti-Bullying Committee a good idea? What might it do? Should training in mediation and conflict resolution skills be provided? If so, how and by whom?
14. What kinds of resources (books and videos) for the school to counter bullying would you recommend?

15. How appealing are the alternative ways of dealing with cases of bullying? Under what circumstances, if any, would you see each of the ones suggested being employed? Is additional understanding and training in particular methods needed? If so, how can it be obtained?

16. Should the severity of the bullying and the reasons for the bullying behaviour be taken into account when dealing with the perpetrators?

17. How can children who bully be helped to lead more pro-social lives?

18. How can one ensure that children who are repeatedly victimised receive appropriate help, without matters being made worse?

19. How can one make sure that parents are included in the development of policy to counter bullying?

20. How can school and parents best work together constructively, when cases of bullying occur, and assure the safety of children?

Questionnaire for Young Children

Here are some questions for you to answer. Your teacher will help you in understanding what you have to do. (Teachers: please make overheads of the pictures to help to show how children can respond.)

Are you a boy or a girl? ....

How old are your? ....

What year of school are you now in? ....

Now look at these faces, which face is most like you when you are at school? (Circle the letter near the face most like yours)

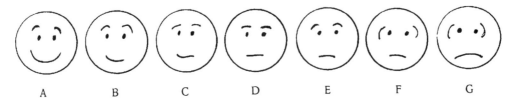

Look at these 3 pictures. Then circle the letter (A, B of C) most like you at playtime?

Picture 1

Picture 2

Picture 3

A   B   C

Have you ever told a teacher that another student or students have tried to hurt you?
(Circle 'yes' or 'no')

Have you ever tried to hurt another person at school who was not as strong as you are?

Yes, lots of times   Sometimes   Never

What is the nicest thing about your school?

_____

_____

_____

_____

_____

Questionnaire for older students

Please answer these questions about your life at school. There is no need to give your name

Year of class ...... Your age in years...... Your sex ......

1. How well do you get on with students at this school? (Circle one of the following)

| Always well | Usually well | Well about half the time | Usually not well | Never well |

We are interested in what bullying goes on in this school. We call it bullying when people deliberately and repeatedly threaten or hurt a less powerful person by what they do or say.

2. Has you ever been bullied by another students or group of this year? (Circle one)

Yes   No

3. If you have answered "yes", indicate how often each of the following has happened to year this (Circle "never" "sometimes" or "never" in each case)

I have been hit or threatened	Never	Sometimes	Often
I have been called unpleasant names	Never	Sometimes	Often
I have been deliberately left out of things by others	Never	Sometimes	Often

4. How have you felt about being bullied by others? (Circle one answer)

| I was never bullied by anyone | I was bullied but not bothered by it | I was bothered a bit by it | I was upset good deal |

5. Do you personally feel safe from being bullied at this school? (Circle your answer)

| Always | Usually | Half the time | Usually feel unsafe | Never feel safe |

6. Could you use some help to stop the bullying? (Circle your answer)

Yes   Unsure   No

Thank you very much

Questionnaire for staff on school peer relations

This is a brief questionnaire for which no personal details are required

The focus in this questionnaire is on bullying which can be described as occurring when people deliberately and repeatedly threaten or hurt a less powerful person by what they do or say

1. What is your judgement of the extent of bullying at this school between students in the following way?: (Circle your answer)

Students are bullied by being hit or threatened by others	Never	Sometimes	Often
Students are bullied by being called unpleasant names	Never	Sometimes	Often
Students are bullied by being deliberately left out of things by others	Never	Sometimes	Often

2. How safe do you think children feel at this school from being bullied by other students? (Circle your answer)

Always feel Safe	Usually feel safe	Half the time feel safe	Usually feel unsafe	Never feel safe

3. Personally do you ever feel seriously bullied by any of the following this year? (Circle any or none of the them)

Teaching staff	students	parents	administrators

4. Do you think it is, or would be, a good idea ? (Circle your answer)

a.	To have a specific policy addressing bullying at the school?	Yes	No
b.	For teachers to talk to students about bullying?	Yes	No
c.	For students to be trained to be peer helpers to assist in? countering bullying?	Yes	No
d.	For the parents of children involved in bully/victim problems to be interviewed by staff	Yes	No

5. Finally how serious do you think the problem of bullying in schools really is? (Circle your answer)

Very serious	serious	moderately serious	not very serious	not serious at all

Questionnaire for Parents

We are interested in making sure that our school is a place where students can enjoy good relations with others. We want to know how you see your child relating to other students at school and in particular whether you think he or she ever experiences any bullying or harassment there. We would also appreciate your getting views on this matter. We have prepared this short questionnaire so that you can help us with our plans to ensure that this is a safe and happy school.

If you have more than one child at this school, please fill in a copy of this questionnaire for each of them.

Sex of child ……….. Age of child ……….. Year of schooling ……………

Would you say your child enjoys good relations with other students at school? (Tick one)

Yes , always or nearly always
Usually does
About half the time
Usually does not
Never or hardly ever

We may say children are being bullied if they are deliberately and repeatedly threatened or hurt by another person or group of people who are more powerful than themselves.

Would you say that your child has been bullied **this year** by a student or group of students in any of these ways; (Circle your answer)

By being threatened or physically hit	Never	Sometimes	Often
By being called unpleasant names	Never	Sometimes	Often
By being deliberately excluded	Never	Sometimes	Often

How has your child been affected by bullying this year (Circle one)

Not affected at all   Has been bothered by it   Has been upset by it

Has your child ever stayed home because of bullying? (Circle your answer)

Never   For a day or so   For more than a day   I don't know

Do you think the school should have a specific anti- bullying policy? (Circle one)

Yes   No   Unsure

Please add any comments you would like to make about the problem of bullying. We would welcome your opinion.

Warning signs that a child is being bullied at school

There are some signs that suggest that a child may be being bullied at school. Parents should inquire as to whether the child is being bullied if these signs are present:

Physical

- Unexplained bruises, scratches or cuts
- Torn or damaged clothes or belongings

Psychosomatic

- Non-specific pains, headaches, abdominal pains

Behavioural

- Fear of walking to or from school
- Change of route to school
- Asking to be driven to school
- Unwilling to go to school
- Deterioration in school work
- Coming home starving (because lunch money was taken)
- "Loss" of possessions/pocket money
- Asking for or stealing money (to pay the bully)
- Having few friends
- Rarely invited to parties

Change in behaviour

- Become withdrawn
- Stammer
- Unexpected mood change
- Irritability and temper outbursts
- Appear upset, unhappy, tearful, distressed
- Stop eating
- Attempt suicide
- Appear anxious: may wet bed, bite nails, seem afraid, develop tic, sleep poorly, cry out in sleep
- Refuse to say what is wrong
- Give improbable excuses or explanations for any of the above

From: Rigby, K. (1996) **Bullying in Schools and What to do about it**, Camberwell, ACER. (Adapted from Dr. Judith Dawkins) Available in the UK from Jessica Kingsley Publishers.

Bystander Exercise

Here is a picture of a person being bullied with a number of people watching. The person being pushed down is the victim; the person pushing the kid down is the bully.

1. How often does this kind of thing happen at your school? Place a tick under your answer.

Every day	Most days of The week	Once or twice a week	Less than once a week	Hardly ever
☐	☐	☐	☐	☐

2. Now please place a tick against what you think you would do if you were watching what was happening. Tick only **one**:

☐ I would ignore it

☐ I would support the person being pushed down

☐ I would support the person who is pushing the other kid down

☐ I would get a teacher

3. Write a sentence saying why you ticked the one you did

_____

_____

_____

_____

_____

Quiz about bullying

Answer by circling "agree" or "unsure" or "disagree" in each case

1.	Bullying is the same thing as fighting	Agree	Unsure	Disagree
2.	Boys usually bully more than girls	Agree	Unsure	Disagree
3.	Kids who are not physically strong always get bullied	Agree	Unsure	Disagree
4.	Telling someone you have been bullied usually makes things worse for you	Agree	Unsure	Disagree
5.	Bullying mostly happens when no-one else is around	Agree	Unsure	Disagree
6.	Most bullying by boys is physical	Agree	Unsure	Disagree
7.	Being bullied repeatedly can make a person depressed	Agree	Unsure	Disagree
8.	Some children who have been severely bullied have taken their own lives	Agree	Unsure	Disagree
9.	Calling people names can be bullying	Agree	Unsure	Disagree
10.	Girls are more likely than boys to bully people by deliberately excluding them	Agree	Unsure	Disagree
11.	You can always stop a person from bullying you by hitting back	Agree	Unsure	Disagree
12.	Sometimes when you are being teased it will stop if you ignore it	Agree	Unsure	Disagree
13.	When students at school see bullying going on they usually try to stop it	Agree	Unsure	Disagree
14.	Bullies generally think badly of themselves	Agree	Unsure	Disagree
15.	Some children are bullied because of their race	Agree	Unsure	Disagree
16.	Some children are bullied because of a disability they have, such as stammering	Agree	Unsure	Disagree
17.	What schools do can never reduce bullying	Agree	Unsure	Disagree
18.	Some children are more inclined to bully than others	Agree	Unsure	Disagree
19.	Children who are bullied a lot tend to have few friends	Agree	Unsure	Disagree
20.	Once a bully always a bully	Agree	Unsure	Disagree

Answers to the quiz

The quiz was devised to help teachers open up a discussion about bullying in classes. The answers given below are based upon the views of most researchers who have studied bullying in schools. They may nevertheless be questioned; future research may lead to different viewpoints.

1. Disagree
2. Agree
3. Disagree
4. Disagree
5. Disagree
6. Disagree
7. Agree
8. Agree
9. Agree
10. Agree
11. Disagree
12. Agree
13. Disagree
14. Disagree
15. Agree
16. Agree
17. Disagree
18. Agree
19. Agree
20. Disagree

This quiz is taken from *Stop the bullying: a handbook for schools* (Canadian edition, forthcoming) by Ken Rigby.